THE WARFARE OF
THE SPIRIT

The Warfare of the Spirit

A.W. Tozer

Compiled by Harry Verploegh

CHRISTIAN PUBLICATIONS
CAMP HILL, PENNSYLVANIA

Christian Publications, Inc.
3825 Hartzdale Drive
Camp Hill, PA 17011

www.christianpublications.com

Faithful, biblical publishing since 1883

The Warfare of the Spirit
ISBN: 0-87509-545-3

LOC Control Number: 93-72164

Unless otherwise indicated, Scripture is taken from the Holy Bible:
King James Version.

CONTENTS

Foreword   1

1   *The Warfare of the Spirit   3*

2   *The Money Question Needs Prayerful
Restudy—Part I   5*

3   *The Money Question needs Prayerful
Restudy—Part II   9*

4   *Are We Evangelicals Social Climbing?   13*

5   *Crowning the Court Fool   17*

6   *Let No One Become Necessary to You   20*

7   *The Art of Doing Good Unobtrusively
—Part I   24*

8   *The Art of Doing Good Unobtrusively
—Part II   29*

9   *What Made David Run?   33*

10   *Eternal Retribution—A Bible Doctrine   37*

11   *A Word to the Wise   42*

12   *Eating the Locoweed   46*

13   *Perfect Love Casts Out Fear   50*

14   *Christmas Reformation Long Overdue   54*

15   *Lift You Glad Voices   58*

16   *Laboring the Obvious   63*

17   *Ability and Responsibility   68*

18   *Beware the Romantic Spirit in Religion   73*

19 Joy Will Come in Its Own Time   77

20 Temperance, the Rare Virtue   81

21 The Dangers of Overstimulation   86

22 The Meaning of Christmas   90

23 A Glance Back and a Look Foward   94

24 Singing Commentary   98

25 Our Imperfect View of Truth   102

26 The Easter Emphasis   107

27 The Teachings of Christ Are for Christians   111

28 The Decline of Good Reading   115

29 The Way of the Cross   119

30 Needed: A Reformation within the Church   123

31 The Perils of Too Much Liberty   128

32 The Days of Our Years   133

33 On Going through School without
     Learning Anything   138

34 The Deadliest Sins of All   142

35 Conformity, a Snare in Religion   146

36 The Popularity of Christ   151

37 The Lordship of the Man Jesus Is Basic   156

38 The Menace of the Common Image   161

39 Satan's Defeat Linked to His Moral Folly   165

40 The Man and the Machine   169

41 Leaders and Followers   173

Foreword

We children of Ada Pfautz Tozer and Aiden Wilson Tozer are grateful to God for each of them. They gave us a rich Christian heritage, sound teaching and constant self-sacrifice. While many continue to appreciate the writings and sermons of A.W. Tozer at a distance, we saw at home, up close, how sincerely they believed the truths he preached and how determined they both were to live the life of the Spirit.

Our mother's counsel and self-sacrifice and her help and encouragement were essential to his work. He could not have lived as he lived or worked as he did had she not been patient and strong and willing to take the heavy end of the life of our boisterous home. Her sweet disposition and bright smile, her hospitality, and her love and friendliness to all around her made our home happy and our lives secure.

Our parents gave us a home centered on Christ and the Bible with the church a large part of our life. At dinner on Sundays after church, we were invited to comment on the sermon and, no matter how half-baked our comments, they were listened to and discussed as though they were important. Discussion of Scripture, of music, great literature, some other branch of learning or something so simple as the derivation of an English word usually followed. The conversation was serious but always filled with humor and light banter to keep everyone participating. Our parents worked the gathering as a team; she fluttering around making sure everyone was heard and none was hurt; he pouncing on flawed logic and poking fun at any "sophomoric" ideas of their over-educated children.

Their guidance was not by pressure or rigid rules but by respect and high expectation, open conversation, love and living example, always keeping before us the things that matter now and will matter in the world to come.

We are grateful to have been given this opportunity, on the occasion of the publication of this last in the series of collections of our father's editorials, to acknowledge publicly the debt we owe to God for our parents.

Lowell, Forrest, Aiden Jr., Wendell,
Raleigh, Stanley, Rebecca

The Warfare of the Spirit

There is a kind of dualism in our fallen world which has accounted for most of the persecutions endured by believers since the days of Cain and Abel.

There are two spirits in the earth, the Spirit of God and the spirit of Satan, and these are at eternal enmity. The ostensible cause of religious hatred may be almost anything; the true cause is nearly always the same: the ancient animosity which Satan, since the time of his inglorious fall, has ever felt toward God and His kingdom. Satan is aflame with desire for unlimited dominion over the human family; and whenever that evil ambition is challenged by the Spirit of God, he invariably retaliates with savage fury.

The world hated Jesus without a cause. In spite of their fantastic charges against Him, Christ's contemporaries found nothing in either His doctrines or His deeds to rouse in them such unreasonable anger as they constantly displayed toward Him. They hated Him, not for anything He said or did, but for what He was.

It is possible within the provisions of redemptive grace to enter into a state of union with Christ so perfect that the world will instinctively react toward us exactly as it did toward Him in the days of His flesh.

It is a great reproach to us as Christians that we excite in the hearts of the unbelieving masses little more than plain boredom. They meet us with smiling toleration or ignore us altogether, and their silence is a portent and a sign. Well might it cause us nights of tears and hours of prayerful self-examination.

It is the Spirit of Christ in us that will draw Satan's fire. The people of the world will not much care what we believe and they will stare vacantly at our religious forms, but there is one thing they will never forgive us—the presence of God's Spirit in our hearts. They may not know the cause of that strange feeling of antagonism which rises within them, but it will be nonetheless real and dangerous. Satan will never cease to make war on the Man-child, and the soul in which dwells the Spirit of Christ will continue to be the target for his attacks.

The Money Question Needs Prayerful Restudy—Part I

The question of money and its place in the church is calling for a prayerful restudy in the light of the Holy Scriptures. The whole matter should be reappraised and adjusted to conform to the teachings of Christ.

If the New Testament is, as we claim it to be, the source of all we are to believe about spiritual things, then there is real reason to be disturbed over the present financial practices among evangelical churches. For the moment I am thinking not about the use the individual Christian makes of his money, but about the place money holds in the thought and practices of organized Christian churches and societies.

Christian truth is to be found not in the letter only, but in the mood and spirit of the New Testa-

ment as well. Our Lord's life on earth was as re-
vealing as His words. How he felt about things,
the values He placed upon them, His sympathies,
His antipathies, sometimes tell us as much as His
more formal teachings.

One truth we may learn from His life as well as
from His doctrine is that earthly riches cannot pro-
cure human happiness. It is hard for a rich church to
understand that her Lord was a poor man. Were He
to appear today on our city streets as He appeared
in Jerusalem, He would in all probability be picked
up for vagrancy. Were He to teach here what He
taught the multitudes about money, He would be
blacklisted by churches, Bible conferences and missionary societies everywhere as unrealistic, fanatical
and dangerous to organized religion.

Our Lord simply did not think about money
the way His professed followers do today; and
more particularly He did not give it the place our
religious leaders give it. To them it is necessary; to
Him it was not. He had nowhere to lay His head,
and we have made poetry out of His poverty
while being extremely careful not to share it. We
have explained away His clear declaration that it
is impossible for a rich man to enter the kingdom
of heaven. We have commingled the teaching of
Christ with the teachings of Benjamin Franklin
and the dollar-sign philosophers which America
has produced in such abundance, and Christ's
teachings have lost their meaning for us.

Church finances are a good and proper part of
church life, but there is an ever-present danger

that they will grow too important in the thinking of the church officers and slowly crowd out more vital things. In our local assemblies and other evangelical organizations there are signs that should disturb us greatly, signs of degeneration and decay that can only lead to spiritual death if the infection is not discovered and checked.

To be specific, some of our religious leaders appear to have developed mercantile minds and have come to judge all things by their effect upon the church finances. What a church can or cannot do is decided by the state of the treasury. Its spiritual outgo is determined by its financial income, with no margin for miracle and no recognition of a spiritual ministry unrelated to money. Such evil practice results from an erroneous attitude toward the whole financial question as it relates to religion.

It is an ominous thing in any church when the treasurer begins to exercise power. Since he may be presumed to be a man of God he should have a place equal to that of any other member, and if he is a man of gifts and virtues he will naturally have certain influences among the brethren. This is right and normal as long as he exercises his influences as a man of God and not as a treasurer. The moment he becomes important *because* he is treasurer, the Spirit will be grieved and His manifestations will begin to diminish. Then will follow coldness and spiritual sterility which we will try desperately to cure by wild appeals to God for revival. That the revival never comes is due altogether to the fact that we are violating the laws of God and forcing the Spirit to withdraw His power from us.

Again, it is a sign and a portent when a member is cultivated for his generosity and given a place of eminence in the church out of proportion to his spiritual gifts and graces. To court a Christian for his financial contributions is as evil a thing as to marry a man for his money. To flatter a man for any reason whatever is to degrade ourselves and imperil his soul. To flatter a man because he is a heavy giver is to offer him a concealed affront as well, for back of the purring and the smirking is the hidden opinion that the man's money is more important than the man and more to be esteemed.

The Bible has much to say about money and its place in the work and worship of the church. It is possible to bring our thinking and practice into accord with the will of God in this matter as in all others.

The Money Question Needs Prayerful Restudy—Part II

C hrist likened His followers to children and sheep and pointed to birds and lilies as having valuable lessons for us.

These four little creatures differ widely from each other, but have one thing in common: their complete freedom from worry. They have no financial troubles. They live spontaneously, simply, without strain, and God takes care of them. This is what our Lord wants us to learn to do as individual Christians, and the same spirit should characterize every church and every Christian institution of whatever sort it may be.

We in the churches seem unable to rise above the fiscal philosophy which rules the business world; so we introduce into our church finances the psychology of the great secular institutions so familiar to us all and judge a church by its financial report much as we judge a bank or a department store.

A look into history will quickly convince any interested person that the true church has almost always suffered more from prosperity than from poverty. Her times of greatest spiritual power have usually coincided with her periods of indigence and rejection; with wealth came weakness and backsliding. If this cannot be explained, neither apparently can it be escaped. People simply run true to their nature; and after all the church is composed of people.

It is a well-known fact that authority requires money to maintain itself in power, and it is not otherwise when that authority is ecclesiastical. The economic squeeze is not unknown in religious circles and has always been the devil's own device whether used by a church board to bring a bold pastor to time or by denominational leaders to force a local church into line. Such abuses are possible only because we have allowed ourselves to get entangled in unscriptural methods of church financing.

The point I am trying to make here is that while money has a proper place in the total life of the church militant, the tendency is to attach to it an importance that is far greater than is biblically sound or morally right. The average church has so established itself organizationally and financially that God is simply not necessary to it. So entrenched is its authority and so stable are the religious habits of its members that God could withdraw Himself completely from it as it could run on for years on its own momentum. And the same is true of schools, Bible conferences and missionary societies.

It is particularly regrettable that the activities of churches and societies must be cut back to agree with actual or anticipated income. Think back to the roots of this practice and you will see that it makes the power of the Spirit of God depend upon the state of the national economy or the varying wage levels in different localities. Should the members of a local church withhold their tithes and offerings that church will accomplish less statistically, it is true, but always its accomplishments will depend upon its spiritual condition and not upon its treasury. The treasury will be full if the people are holy; or if the people are generous but poor, then the Holy Spirit will give them fruit out of all proportion to their financial report. The fruit of the church agrees with its basic spirituality, never upon the state of its exchequer.

The history of churches and denominations follows pretty closely a rather uniform pattern: It is to begin in poverty and power; get established to a degree that removes all hazard and gives financial security; become accepted by society; outgrow the need for divine intervention; keep Christ as a figurehead, ignore His Lordship and carry on after the traditions of the elders; offer the clergy a reward for staying in line in the form of an old age pension; put enough persons in places of power who profit financially by the prosperity of the group. After that it's *requiescat in pace*,* and the tragic thing about it all is that no one knows he is dead.

No church or denomination need go that way if the members detect the trend before it is too late. But I wonder. So bound are we to the treasurer's report that we habitually forget who we are and what we are called to do. Anyone can do the possible; add a bit of courage and zeal and some may do the phenomenal; only Christians are obliged to do the impossible. If we could rise in faith like Samson and break the ropes that bind us we might see again that a church's outgo can be greater than its income, as much greater as God is greater than circumstances. We might have demonstrated before our eyes how God works wonders when His people leave a margin for miracles.

*a prayer for the peaceful repose of a dead person

Are We Evangelicals Social Climbing?

Traditionally Christianity has been the religion of the common people. Whenever the upper classes have adopted it in numbers, it has died. Respectability has almost always proved fatal to it.

The reasons back of this are two, one human and the other divine.

Schleiermacher has pointed out that at the bottom of all religion there lies a feeling of dependence, a sense of creature helplessness. The simple man who lives close to the earth lives also close to death and knows that he must look for help beyond himself; he knows that there is but a step between him and catastrophe. As he rises in the social and economic scale, he surrounds himself with more and more protective devices and pushes danger (so he thinks) farther and farther from him. Self-confidence displaces the feeling of dependence he once knew and God becomes less necessary to him. Should he stop to think this through he would know better than to place his confidence in things and people; but so badly are we injured by our moral fall that we are capable of deceiving ourselves completely and, if conditions favor it, to keep up the deception for a lifetime.

Along with the feeling of security that wealth and position bring comes an arrogant pride that shuts tightly the door of the heart to the waiting Savior. Our Very Important Man may indeed honor a church by joining it, but there is no life in his act. His religion is external and his faith nominal. Conscious respectability has destroyed him.

The second reason Christianity tends to decline as its devotees move up the social scale is that God will not respect persons nor share His glory with another. Paul sets this forth plainly enough in his First Corinthians epistle:

> Because the foolishness of God is wiser than men; and the weakness of God is stronger than men. For ye see your calling, brethren, how that not many wise men after the flesh, not many mighty, not many noble, are called: But God hath chosen the foolish things of the world to confound the wise; and God hath chosen the weak things of the world to confound the things which are mighty; And base things of the

world, and things which are despised,
hath God chosen, yea, and things which
are not, to bring to nought things that are:
That no flesh should glory in his presence.
(1 Corinthians 1:25–29)

When God sent His Son to redeem mankind He
sent Him to the home of a working man and He
grew up to be what we now call a peasant. When
He presented Himself to Israel and launched into
His earthly ministry, He was rejected by the respectable religionists and had to look for followers almost exclusively from among the poor, plain
people. When the Spirit came and the church was
founded, its first members were the socially unac-
ceptable. For generations the church drew her
numbers from among the lower classes, individual exceptions occurring now and again, of which
Saul of Tarsus was the most noteworthy.

During the centuries since Pentecost the path
of true Christianity has paralleled pretty closely
the path Jesus walked when He was here on
earth: it was to be rejected by the great and accepted by the lowly. The institutionalized church
has certainly not been poor, nor has she lacked for
great and mighty men to swell her membership.
But this great church has had no power. Almost
always the approval of God has rested upon small
and marginal groups whose members were
scorned while they lived and managed to gain acceptance only after they had been safely dead
several score years.

Today we evangelicals are showing signs that we are becoming too rich and too prominent for our own good. With a curious disregard for the lessons of history we are busy fighting for recognition by the world and acceptance by society. And we are winning both. The great and the mighty are now looking our way. The world seems about to come over and join us. Of course we must make some concessions, but these have almost all been made already except for a bit of compromising here and there on such matters as verbal inspiration, special creation, separation and religious tolerance.

Evangelical Christianity is fast becoming the religion of the bourgeoisie. The well-to-do, the upper middle classes, the politically prominent, the celebrities are accepting our religion by the thousands and parking their expensive cars outside our church doors, to the uncontrollable glee of our religious leaders who seem completely blind to the fact that the vast majority of these new patrons of the Lord of glory have not altered their moral habits in the slightest nor given any evidence of true conversion that would have been accepted by the saintly fathers who built the churches.

Yes, history is a great teacher, but she cannot teach those who do not want to learn. And apparently we do not.

Crowning the Court Fool

I n olden days they crowned the king and tied a cap and bell on the court fool; today we crown the fool and tie a tin can on the king.

The court fool, as every reader of history knows, was a professional jester or comedian retained at court to provide the king some comic relief from the serious and sometimes dangerous business of ruling the country.

This ancient jester, or fool, occupied a unique position which he won by his quick wit and his talent for amusing people. He was loved for his ability to convulse a dignified assembly with his sidesplitting humor, sometimes aimed at one of the great men present or even at the king himself, though it was a bit risky to make the king the butt of a joke, for the jester never knew whether his majesty would accept it good-naturedly and laugh with the rest or have him whipped and thrown into prison for his impertinence. At best he was treated with the affection shown to a house pet; at worst he was kicked and cuffed about, either because his wit was too pointed or because he couldn't think of anything funny when his royal boss called for it.

Seeing that we humans were once created in the image of God and that we have by our sin fallen into a state of spiritual blindness and mortality, I would rather be a serious-minded dolt concerned about eternal life than to be an overpaid jester with nothing better to do than to make men laugh and forget that they must die and come to judgment.

It is surely an incredible state of affairs when the entertainer rates higher in public esteem than the doctor, the nurse, the teacher and the statesman upon whose shoulders rest the hopes of whole generations of men. Yet it is so today in our ostensibly civilized society. In America the court fool now wears the crown and rules over the minds of millions of chortling subjects who want nothing higher or better in this life than to kick off their shoes and spend an evening of howling mirth over the hoary chestnuts dished out by the current royal jester, whoever he may happen to be.

That his sidesplitting witticisms were written for him by others and read by him from a script never seems to tarnish his golden crown in the eyes of his adoring subjects. He still takes his willing tribute from the masses who would rather roar with ill-advised laughter than to weep over their sins.

Yes, we have crowned the fool and spurned the real kings among us: The farmer who toils for us from sunup to sundown, the teacher who gets old and tired trying to make ladies and gentlemen out of the boys and girls we place in their care, the doctor who brought those boys and girls into the world and who stands to watch over their health while they grow up, the corner policeman who brings at least a semblance of safety to our streets, the soldier whose blood has bought our American soil a hundred times during the years of our history, the patriotic statesman who labors to make and keep our country free. These are underpaid, overlooked and generally tolerated while the court fool struts about over the world as if he were a king indeed instead of the cheap jester that he is.

There isn't likely to be much of a change soon. I am not so naive as to think that my protest here will alter affairs in this sin-ridden and habit-bound world; but I have hope that the children of God will understand. Often Christians themselves do not notice such things until they are pointed out to them.

Let No One Become Necessary to You

E very believer has had or will sometime have the experience of leaning hard on the example of someone wiser and more spiritual than himself and looking to him for counsel and guidance in the Christian life.

This is good and scriptural and not to be condemned. Happy is the newborn babe in Christ who can find a pure and holy soul whom he can take as a model and from whom he can learn the ways of the kingdom. Such a one can act as a mentor to save the young Christian from many mistakes and pitfalls into which he otherwise might fall.

Much is said about this in the Scriptures and many examples are found there. Joshua had his Moses, Elisha had his Elijah and Timothy his Paul. It speaks well of the humility of the younger men that they were willing to learn and of the patience of the older ones that they were willing to teach. Had Moses, for instance, withdrawn his company and refused to be bothered with the young Joshua the history of Israel would have been different, as it would have been also if Joshua had been too proud and self-assured to sit at the feet of Moses.

The master-disciple relationship is normal and wholesome up to a given point; after that it becomes harmful both to the master and to the disciple. A tiny babe at the breast is a beautiful and natural thing to see, but a four-year-old child that has not been weaned is doing injury to itself physically and psychologically. Such an abnormality would reflect on the child's intelligence and on the competence and wisdom of the mother.

Elisha followed Elijah till he had learned from him all the old man could teach him; then God took Elijah away and the young man was on his own. The finest compliment to Elijah's ability as a spiritual teacher was paid by none less than the Lord Himself when He took the teacher to heaven and left the disciple to carry on without him. The old man of God had done his work well and the younger man needed him no more.

This kind of thing has been repeated innumerable times down the centuries; the teacher makes himself unnecessary and passes on and the disciple stands upright and begins to walk with no one to lean on. This is as it should be, for the teacher cannot stay always. Time carries him away and the cause of truth must be served by those whom he has taught and inspired while he walked among them. Has he failed to teach well or has the disciple failed to learn, the work of God will falter and halt and the world be poorer as a consequence.

To the one who is advanced enough to hear it I would say, *never let anyone become necessary to you.* Be meek enough to learn from the lowly and wise enough to learn from the enlightened. Be quick to profit by the experiences of others and stay alert to the voice of wisdom from whatever direction it may sound. As the bee soars for nectar where the blossoms are thickest, so you must search for spiritual nectar where it is most likely to be found, which is among those Christians who are the most consecrated, the most prayerful and the most experienced.

Every man has some contributions to make to your life if you know how to receive it; certain men will astonish you with their ability to answer your unexpressed question and tell you what is in your heart. But never attach yourself to any man as a parasite. Adopt no man as a *guru.* Apart from the inspired writers of Holy Scriptures no man is worthy of such confidence. The sweetest saint can be mistaken.

I repeat, never let any man become necessary to you. Christ alone is necessary. Apart from Him we are completely wretched; without Him we cannot live and dare not die. Our need of Him is real and vital and will outlast time and go on into eternity. That deep and desperate need is met by Christ so completely that when we have Him we need no one else. We may receive help from our fellow Christians as they from us, but our need for them is relative and fleeting. Let anyone become spiritually indispensable to us and we have deserted the Rock to build on shifting sand.

It requires deep consecration, I admit, and complete detachment from earthly interests to reach such a place of independence. And it is only after we become completely dependent upon God that we can walk without leaning on men. It takes much prayer and quiet contemplation to maintain the nice balance that will permit us to receive help from our fellow Christians and at the same time be sweetly independent of them. But we should not despair; it is not beyond the possibilities of grace. Not even for such weak Christians as we are.

The Art of Doing Good
Unobtrusively—Part I

We Are Called to Do Good

From the Bible and from the example of Christ it is clear that Christians are here on earth to do good.

One passage tells us that Christ "went about doing good, and healing all that were oppressed of the devil; for God was with him" (Acts 10:38). In addition to His healing ministry and His work of instructing in the truth, He engaged in another kind of activity which the Spirit calls simply "doing good."

"As he is, so are we in this world" (1 John 4:17b). We who call ourselves by His name are under obligation to imitate Him in His deeds of kindness.

In current Christian teaching it is usually as-
sumed that the works we are called to do are miracles. It is a lot easier to apply every passage that
speaks of good works to something big and dramatic than to accept it as meaning some plain,
humble task of mercy such as clothing the naked
and feeding the hungry. We of the evangelical
fold are much more easily persuaded to pray all
night for God to do a miracle than to put on our
work clothes and help a neighbor.

Without doubt there are activities that take pre-
cedence over works of charity. One is the work of
witnessing to the grace and power of God as expressed through Jesus Christ. This is set forth in
Acts 1:8, "But ye shall receive power, after that the
Holy Ghost is come upon you: and ye shall be witnesses unto me."

A second work the Christian is called upon to
do is that of setting a holy example before an unholy world.

> Ye are the light of the world. . . . Let your
> light so shine before men, that they may see
> your good works, and glorify your father
> which is in heaven. (Matthew 5:14a, 16)

In accord with this Paul exhorted his friend
Timothy, "Let no man despise thy youth; but be
thou an example of the believers, in word, in conversation, in faith, in purity" (1 Timothy 4:12).

The third responsibility the Christian has toward his fellow believer and toward the world is
to do, in the language of another, "all the good

you can, to all the people you can, in all the ways you can, as long as ever you can."

The Scriptures present a charming picture of the ideal woman, and one feature present is the practice of good works. Lemuel's description of a virtuous woman in the thirty-first chapter of Proverbs shows us one who is not only morally pure, but hard working and industrious too, and along with her housewifely activities she manages also to do many good works for others: "She stretcheth out her hand to the poor; yea, she reacheth forth her hands to the needy" (Proverbs 31:20). Paul required that the women believers in the early Church "adorn themselves" with modest apparel and good works (1 Timothy 2:9–10). Before an elderly woman could be "put on the list of widows" (obviously received into the first Christian home for the aged), it had to be shown not only that she had professed to be a Christian but that she was "well reported of for good works; if she have brought up children, if she have lodged strangers, if she have washed the saints' feet, if she have relieved the afflicted, if she have diligently followed every good work" (5:10).

The test of good works, which Paul laid down for the women, applies as well to men. In a passage obviously addressed to men the apostle exhorts that they

> Charge them that are rich in this world, that they be not highminded, nor trust in uncertain riches, but in the living God, who giveth us richly all things to enjoy;

That they do good, that they be rich in good works, ready to distribute, willing to communicate. (6:17–18)

Some Christians feel little or no sympathy for those outside the fold. Let it be suggested that help be granted to some unfortunate human and the question is instantly asked, "Is he a Christian?" or "Is he worthy of our assistance?"

This attitude is wrong for a number of reasons and altogether beneath those who call themselves by the sacred name of Christ. If we are to help only the worthy, who then can qualify? The Christian can hide his goods away with a pure conscience, safe in the knowledge that he would help the poor if he could find any worthy of it. The moth and rust would qualify, to be sure, and they will get them at last; in the meantime the happy believer can sing hymns and distribute tracts while the poor ask for bread and there is none and little children cry themselves to sleep at night with no one to comfort them.

In the sixth chapter of his Galatian epistle Paul settled forever the scope of our Christian responsibility: "As we have therefore opportunity, let us do good unto all men, especially unto them who are of the household of faith" (Galatians 6:10). This is in harmony with the truth found in the widely known story of the Good Samaritan, where it is established that our "neighbor" is anyone who needs us, whether or not he is of our kin or nationality. I do not see how we can escape the force of this double witness; and to tell the truth, I do not believe any honest person can.

That we should do good in Christ's name no one can deny. How to do it without letting our right hand know what our left hand is doing (Matthew 6:3) is an art not many have managed to learn.

The Art of Doing Good Unobtrusively—Part II

The Left Hand and the Right

In searching the Holy Scriptures two facts need to be faced squarely: One is that in the body of revealed truth there are no real contradictions; the other, that contradictions do sometimes appear to be present.

To admit contradictions is to deny the infallibility of the Word; to deny that they seem to be there is to be unrealistic and put ourselves at the mercy of our enemies.

In our Lord's teachings concerning good works, for instance, it is easy to find apparent inconsistencies. In Matthew 5:16 He says plainly, "Let your light so shine before men, that they may see your good works, and glorify your father which is in heaven." The words "that they may see" can only mean that it is His purpose to exhibit the righteous lives of His people before the unrighteous world, and the words "and glorify your Father in heaven" tell us why He wants thus to exhibit them. It is that He may provide an example of godliness which will exercise strong moral influence upon persons who would otherwise not be affected.

That much is easy. The apparent contradiction comes further on when He says, "Take heed that ye do not your alms before men, to be seen of them: otherwise ye have no reward of your Father which is in heaven. But when thou doest alms, let not thy left hand know what thy right hand doeth" (Matthew 6:1, 3).

Here our Lord appears, but only appears, to cancel out His instructions given a few moments before. Bluntly, it would seem that in one place He says "Let" and in the other "Let not." Christ being the incarnation of truth cannot utter contradictions. There must be an explanation which will preserve the organic unity of His teachings and reconcile the two passages. I believe there is.

In one place our Lord speaks of moral conduct, and says in effect, "Go out into the world and live lives so pure and good that your fellow men cannot but see; and when they see they will glorify God who has given such moral power unto men." In the other He says, "Do not make a show of your kind acts. When you help your neighbor, when you minister to the poor, be sure your motive is right. See that your motive is to glorify God and not to earn a cheap reputation as a philanthropist or a heavy giver. Seek not to be known for your generosity, for there lies a snare, and you must by all means avoid it."

From the Scriptures quoted and from countless others we gather truths which may be condensed into this admonition: "Live a pure, righteous life and do not hide it from the world. As much as lies in you, do good to all men, but do it unobtrusively so as not to draw attention to yourself nor bring embarrassment to the one you help."

Unquestionably we are here to do good, but good that is done ostentatiously destroys itself in the doing. Kind acts are fragile things and must be handled carefully if they are not to become unkind and actually injure the one for whom they are performed.

It is possible to donate a large sum of money and lay down terms for its use so dictatorial as to destroy what might otherwise have been a virtuous act. Almost everyone has at some time been amused or disgusted by the well-heeled extrovert who swept up the dinner check with such a satisfied air as made his guest feel under obligation. But over against this I know men who habitually do favors in such a manner as to leave the impression that they and not the recipient are being favored. This is a fine and beautiful art, and one that does not come easily.

The Christian who would have his good works accepted by his Lord will be careful not to tell them abroad, and certainly he will be careful not to boast of them. And we must remember that the neat little disclaimer we hear so often, "I say this to the glory of God," does not change the moral quality of the words that follow. Boasting is boasting, no matter how we dress it.

Again, I have observed how certain moneyed laymen use their generous donations as a kind of gentle blackmail to enable them to retain control of church affairs. And we all know the preacher who allows himself to get so far under obligation to certain of his rich parishoners that he has no independence left. He is their man—bought and paid for—and in their company he dare never again speak all the truth.

It is a spiritual grace to help people without putting them under obligation, without humiliating them and without establishing a superior-inferior relationship. It is an art that can do good casually instead of formally or, as the teenagers say, "making a production out of it."

The world has a saying that if you want to lose a friend, do him a favor. Without doubt this saying is the crystallization of many and bitter experiences in the give and take of human relations.

But could the fault be all on one side? Maybe when we did our friend a favor we adopted a patronizing attitude that struck at his self-respect and stung him to the quick.

Surely of all people we Christians should best know how to receive favors without servility and do good without arrogance. Our Lord was a master of this art; we can learn from Him.

What Made David Run?

A great, a mighty man was this David, son of Jesse the Bethlehemite.

He had ten brothers, but almost nothing is heard of the ten; David alone arrests the pen of inspiration; only David is honored to write as he is moved by the Holy Spirit.

How important a figure he was may be inferred from his refusal to die. David has been gone from the earth about three thousand years; three thousand times the earth has circled around the sun since he left us; three thousand times have the wild geese flown honking toward the south and returned again to the north with the returning spring. Empires have come in to being, run their course and disappeared; thrones have toppled; kings have strutted their little day upon the stage of history and lain down at last to be forgotten or almost forgotten by the world. How many noted men during the long years have come and gone and left no more trace behind them than an arrow leaves when it passes through the air.

Yet David will not die. He served his generation by the will of God and fell asleep, but asleep he has more power over men for good than a thousand religious doctors and bishops do awake. He will not allow oblivion to swallow him nor will he lie quiet with the ancients amid dust and mold. He was a simple shepherd but he stands to teach the learned; he lived an insular life among his own people, but his voice is heard today in almost every land and his pure songs are sung in half a thousand tongues. Scarcely will a church service be held next Sunday anywhere in the world but, unseen, David will direct the choir, and when the minister rises to preach God's truth he will hardly sit down again until he has spoken of David or quoted from his inspired psalms.

What makes David run? Well, I admit to a wealth of ignorance about the whole thing, but if a New Testament Christian may look at an Old Testament king I venture a few words.

Perhaps David's greatness and his significance for mankind lies in his complete preoccupation with God. He was a Jew, steeped in the Levitical tradition, but he never got lost in the forms of religion. "I have set the LORD always before me" (Psalm 16:8), he said once, and again he said, or rather cried, for his words rise from within like a cry, "My soul thirsteth for God, for the living God: when shall I come and appear before God?" (42:2).

David was acutely God-conscious. To him God was the one Being worth knowing. Where others see nature he saw God. He was a nature poet indeed, but he saw God first and loved nature for God's sake. Wordsworth reversed the order and, while he is great, he is not worthy to untie the shoelaces of the man David.

David was also a God-possessed man. He threw himself at the feet of God and demanded to be conquered, and Jehovah responded by taking over his personality and shaping it as a potter shapes the clay.

Because he was God-possessed he could be God-taught. It is scarcely possible to know with any certainty just how great David's educational advantages were, but we may safely assume that he had not much of what we now call formal education. Yet he has taught millions and after the passing of centuries he still keeps school and teaches divine poetry, mystic theology and the art of pure worship to all who have ears to hear.

True, David may have been watching sheep when he should have been in the classroom. That is a guess pure and simple. But it is no guess that he was a student all his days, and neither the care of his sheep when he was a shepherd nor the burden of the nations when he became a king kept him from the purest and noblest of all studies, the study of God. He sent his heart to school to the Most High God, and soon he knew Him with an immediacy of knowing more wonderful than is dreamed of in our philosophies. Jah Jehovah he knew by the Spirit's inward illumination. As the bird knows the thicket where it was hatched or the rabbit the briar patch where it was born, so David knew God with an easy familiarity that was yet sanctified and chastened with godly fear and reverential awe.

What made David run? What makes the child run and shout with glee on a summer morning? What brings the lover to the door where his beloved dwells? David was a God-intoxicated man. He had gazed on God until he was enraptured and that rapture he could not always contain. While still a young man, in the presence of the holy Ark he let himself go in an ecstatic dance that delighted God as much as it outraged the coldhearted Michal.

For many years I had loved the Psalms of David before I knew why. I had returned to them again and again, almost I might say more than to any other portion of Scripture, and I chided myself for this preference for after all I was a New Testament believer and the Psalms belonged to the Old. Then one day I read a sentence from a little book by Horatius Bonar. It said simply, "The Spirit of Jesus dwells in the Psalms." Then I knew and was satisfied.

David in the Spirit knew and communed with the One who was to be his son according to the flesh, "and declared *to be* the Son of God with power, according to the Spirit of holiness, by the resurrection from the dead" (Romans 1:4). It was the love of Christ that made David run. "O love of Jesus! Blessed love!"

Eternal Retribution— A Bible Doctrine

I believe in eternal retribution. That those who continue impenitent to the end of their earthly lives will be banished from the presence of God forever is a truth as clearly taught in the Scriptures as the fall of man or the resurrection of the dead.

The Bible is an organic unity, one with itself throughout, and must be received in toto or in toto rejected. I dare not select the parts I want to believe and exclude what disturbs or offends me. That would be to set up my fallible reason as a criterion against which to judge infallible revelation, obviously in itself an unreasonable thing to do.

While it is true that I stand before the Bible to be judged and not the Bible before me; while it is true that I am morally obliged to accept the Holy

Scriptures and by the light they afford prepare myself so the Holy Scriptures may accept me, as a serious-minded and responsible thinker I must admit that it is sometimes difficult to know precisely what the Scriptures teach on a given subject. When once we know, we must accept and believe; until we know we can maintain our moral integrity only by admitting our ignorance; and that very ignorance itself obliges us to search the Word in prayerful reverence until the light breaks and our doubts are cleared away.

The doctrine of eternal retribution has been held and taught by an overwhelming majority of Christians since the days of the apostles. Almost all, if not quite all, of the church fathers and of the great doctors and saints down the centuries believed that the Bible teaches that the finally impenitent will be cast into a hell from which there is no escape and with no further opportunity to repent and avail themselves of the mercy of God and the benefits of Christ's atonement. They believed, as the vast majority of Bible-loving Christians today believe, that the personality of the impenitent man is perpetuated beyond the moment of physical death, and that the man must face a strict accounting of deeds done on earth and hear the sentence of doom pronounced against him.

I have read the arguments put forth against this belief and acknowledged the force of them, and though my human heart could welcome any gleam of hope, however faint, that might yet remain for the lost, the Scriptures are too plain to allow that hope to exist.

Frederic W. Farrar, the celebrated dean of Canterbury, pleaded with great moral earnestness and overpowering eloquence for what he called "eternal hope" for all men, and like a defense attorney managed to find among the works of the Latin fathers quotations to support that hope. But the weight of evidence on the side of the traditional belief is too great; there can be only one conclusion: the Bible teaches the doctrine of eternal retribution, and every calm, reasonable man will accept the doctrine; or if he rejects it he will reject the Bible along with it. The man who will not believe in hell must surrender his right to believe in heaven.

To keep the whole Christian witness in balance we must teach what the Bible teaches about the future of the impenitent. But we should watch over our own hearts lest, unbeknown to us, we unconsciously welcome the idea of hell as the revenge we take against those who do not believe as we do. Just as the fear of excommunication or purgatory serves to keep the faithful Romanist in line, so it is entirely possible to use the fear of hell to make people knuckle under to the dictatorial pastor or the evangelist trying to fill his quota of converts for the evening.

The idea of hell found in the Scriptures is so fearful that the first impulse of a loving heart is to wish it were not so. But human pity is both a beautiful and a dangerous emotion. Unless it is subjected to the sharp critique of moral judgment it may, and often does, put our sympathies on the side of the murderer instead of on the side of the dead man and the widow and children he has left behind him. Unholy sympathy moves starry-eyed ladies to send flowers to the criminal awaiting execution while the innocent child he may have raped and mutilated scarcely rates a fugitive impulse of pity.

In the same way uninformed and unreasoning sympathy tends to take sides with the fallen and rebellious race of men against the Most High God whose name is Holy. That He gave men life and intelligence, that He has been patient with them while they defied His laws, killed His only begotten Son and scorned His dying love, is overlooked completely. That men use their gift of free will to reject God, choose iniquity and with wide open eyes persistently work to prepare themselves for hell, seems not to matter to some people. In a welter of uncontrollable emotion they throw themselves on the side of God's enemies. This is unbelief masquerading as compassion.

The cry against the idea of moral retribution reveals several deep-lying misconceptions. These have to do with the holiness of God, the nature of man, the gravity of sin and the awesome wonder of the love of God as expressed in redemption. Whoever understands these even imperfectly will take God's side forever, and whatever He may do they will cry with the voice out of the altar, "Even so, Lord God Almighty, true and righteous are thy judgments" (Revelation 16:7).

Perhaps Moody's word about this is as wise as any that has ever been uttered. He said, "No man should preach on hell until he can do it with tears in his eyes."

A Word to the Wise

The job of carrying the gospel to remote tribes hidden in strange and dangerous places often requires a courage and daring equal to that displayed by the explorer in search of a new river or the soldier in the performance of his duties.

There are missionaries who are born adventurers; while wholly consecrated to Christ and utterly devoted to the glory of God, they are for all that very much in love with the physical excitement that accompanies missionary activities in some parts of the world. These have done excellent work and must be classed with the true servants of Christ and messengers of the cross. Their love for lost men is deep and real. Their fondness for travel and danger is natural to them and indeed contributes much to their fittedness for the work they are called to do, a work which their more cautious brethren could never accomplish.

The Christian public, always ready to take the hero to its heart, has shown its amiable weakness by following these men about, to hang breathless on their colorful words and to shower them with money and gifts of every kind. By thus focusing attention upon their task these brethren have done a real favor to the cause of world missions. They have won the prayers and the support of many who would not have been aroused by the ordinary missionary program. Of the purity of their motives and the sincerity of their appeals there can be no doubt. We could use more of such men.

Now it is to be regretted that these men, by their very zeal and by the success of their efforts, have innocently prepared the way for a racket about as neat and lucrative as may be found anywhere within the field of religion. For there have arisen some who do not scruple to exploit the modern Christian's love for color and drama. These have swept in with the sound of a trumpet. They specialize in thrills and tales of adventure both tall and lurid, and in some quarters they have captured the imagination and loyalty of large numbers of Christians of undoubted sincerity.

Without any previous "good report," woefully shy on scholarship, lacking age, experience and wisdom and, in many instances, without having served an apprenticeship to any recognized spiritual leader, they set themselves up as great missionary pioneers and by sheer force of personality manage to extract from an emotional and uncritical public enough money to finance their showy projects.

These depend for their success upon the power of snappy advertising and use every trick in the modern salesman's bag to promote their interests. Missionary work, as they present it, is a huge and enjoyable adventure. Significantly absent are the woes of Calvary and the travail of the Holy Spirit. Their talk is smooth and convincing, but their spirit is not that of the great missionary leaders of the past.

These professional religious adventures may be spotted by one of several marks. One is their everlasting restlessness. They are always turning up in unexpected places with their camera, traveling at the expense of hard-working Christians, of course, and returning to startle the religious public with what their eyes have seen and their camera recorded. Never would they go into a corner of the world's harvest field and lose themselves in the holy work of winning men. It never occurs to them that they should stay on some field and sweat it out after the manner of the great and fruitful missionaries of every society and denomination through the years.

Unfortunately also some religious leaders in the homeland have found that it pays financially to introduce the missionary motif into their program. The public will support a work that has a missionary flavor and these men know it. It is difficult to avoid the conclusion that missions is sometimes used as a bait to bring in crowds and secure increased income.

As painful as it may be to call attention to an abuse like this, it should be done bluntly and fearlessly. Surely it is no proof of Christlikeness to shut our eyes and mouths while a task as sacred as foreign missions suffers at the hands of ambitious and irresponsible men.

Certain types of men only come into focus here. The God-honoring missionary society will be quick to invite inspection of the missionary dollar. But the gay adventurer who wants to go a-roaming at the honest Christian's expense will feel hurt and will no doubt accuse me of attacking the missionary enterprise. Forty years' association with a society where missionaries practice frugality, self-sacrifice, lifelong committal to the task, lonely pioneering, painstaking language study, and where deprivations, dangers and actual martyrdom are accepted as matters of course should acquit me of this charge.

The Christian with money to invest in world evangelization should, as he shall surely face his Lord at the judgment, approach his responsibility carefully. He should demand a reckoning and insist upon knowing how his money is being spent. And he should see to it that he is helping to support only humble and devout men and women who love not their lives unto death. Not one cent should he give to aid the selfish activities of the happy adventurer who seeks to pass for a messenger of Christ.

This whole thing is too sacred to treat lightly; and the judgment is too near.

Eating the Locoweed

In the western United States there grows a plant called the locoweed. It looks like a fern and bears the horrendous botanical name of *astragalus mollissimus.*

This plant is poisonous to cattle and when eaten by a steer has the effect of shorting his equilibrium, destroying his muscular coordination and throwing his eyes out of focus so that he may shy away from the smallest object or misjudge the size of a large object and walk right into the side of a cliff.

I am reliably informed; but since the locoweed is quite obviously outside my field of interest, or at least my sphere of responsibility, I would just skip the whole thing except that it points straight to another and more serious matter which is certainly of critical interest to me. I refer to sin and its effect upon people.

When a steer begins to stagger around after eating the locoweed the rancher knows something is wrong. The beast is not acting like himself. He is, in plain words, loco.

As we consider the potentials for moral greatness that God built into human nature when He made man in His own image; when we see how self-sacrificing and kind people are at their best moments; when we observe the innocent sweetness of a baby or the selfless, shining love of a mother we are scarcely prepared for the shock of reading history or scanning the daily newspaper.

That woman who stands with a smoking pistol in her hand over the body of her murdered husband—can that be the same woman whose face a few hours before was soft and radiant as she nursed her baby at her breast? That boy who plunges a switchblade into the heart of a kid from another part of town—can that be the same boy who before he left the house to join the gang on the corner spent half an hour romping with his little sister or affectionately teasing his mother? That young man who sits grim-faced and silent in the death house awaiting the hour when he must pay for his crimes against the human race—is that the same young man who a few months ago lay face down across the bed and sobbed because a plain little dog he loved had been killed by a car?

While the life of the ordinary person is not so dramatic and violent as those of the persons cited here, his conduct is nevertheless fully as contradictory. He blows hot and cold from day to day;

he is kind and cruel, chaste and lustful, honest and deceitful, generous and covetous; he longs to be good and chooses to be evil, yearns to know God and turns his back upon Him, hopes for heaven and heads toward hell. He is morally loco.

Sin is a poisonous weed that throws the whole nature out of order. The inner life disintegrates; the flesh lusts after forbidden pleasures; the moral judgment is distorted so that often good appears evil and evil good; time is chosen over eternity, earth over heaven and death over life.

This in large measure accounts for the vivid and colorful language employed by the prophets and apostles to describe the effects of sin. "The whole head is sick, and the whole heart faint. From the sole of the foot even unto the head there is no soundness in it; but wounds, and bruises, and putrifying sores" (Isaiah 1:5–6). This is a sample from Isaiah. A dozen pages of quotations equally as strong could be taken from the other prophets and psalmists.

The New Testament is generally thought to be milder than the Old, but we have only to read Christ's indictment of the Pharisees to discover how wrong such a notion is. Peter, John and Jude dip their pens in liquid fire to do justice to the blazing wrath of God against sin, while Paul traces the serpentine path of sin through the human system and proves how confused and morally self-contradictory the heart is that has not been separated from its iniquity.

We must be careful, however, that we do not push our illustration so far as to create the impression that sin is an accident, a disease, a poison unintentionally imbibed. If sin is a disease it is like alcoholism, one that is chosen, bought and voluntarily swallowed. A steer is not responsible for poisoning himself on locoweed, but men are endowed with intelligence and ability to distinguish good from evil; they are therefore not to be excused either for their sin or for the terrible results of it.

Men are indeed accountable for their sins, and their responsibility is twofold. First they are morally obligated to choose the good and reject the evil, and they will be brought to severe and certain judgment for their failure to do it.

Secondly, since God has in Christ provided a cure, they are responsible to humble themselves and seek forgiveness and cleansing at the fountain opened for all men by the hard dying of Jesus Christ on the Roman cross.

"If any man will," said Jesus, and in so saying swept away all excuses and made every man accountable for his future as well as for his past. For in spite of what sin has done to us, we are yet able to exercise a choice unto eternal life; and we are responsible for our choice, whether it be right or wrong.

Perfect Love Casts Out Fear

(Written December 11, 1957)

During the Second World War the Nazis introduced a new weapon which had not been used before, or at least never to the same degree. It was the technique of panic.

Bombs were fitted with eerie whistles that set up an unearthly wail as they sped earthward. This worked well at first. Whole populations rushed out and frantically milled around, getting in each other's way and, what was more serious, blocking the streets and highways and preventing the free passage of troops and ambulances.

This, of course, was the purpose of the scream bomb, to stampede crowds by frightening them. Later the Chinese Reds used this scare technique against U.N. troops in Korea, but it didn't work so well against trained men. They were too hard to scare.

In the present cold war the Soviets are still carrying on the old fear gimmick, issuing veiled warnings and making ominous threats of total destruction of those who stand in their way. The purpose is to break the spirit of free peoples by the psychology of terror. Most of their threats are about as deadly as Halloween masks, and they know that we know it; but they also know that we do not know which one is real, so they keep on trying to panic us.

The nearest we in the United States have come to panic was when the Russians sent up their satellites a few weeks ago. Whether they meant to terrorize us when they hurled their little gadgets into the skies or whether the whole thing was a legitimate scientific venture may never be known for certain, but there can be no doubt that they are now playing the scream bomb game to the limit and enjoying seeing some of the leaders of the greatest and most powerful nation in the world running in terrified circles.

In the lionlike roarings of Mr. Khrushchev some of us detect more than an accidental similarity to the high-pitched screams of the tiger, Hitler. (By the way, I wonder where Hitler is now!)

I have at the moment no advice for the State Department, but I believe I do have a word for God's people. We should keep in mind that no nation is wholly evil, so no sharp national line of demarcation can be drawn between the friends and the enemies of heaven. The free nations of the earth have much for which they should repent, and there are without doubt many true Christians in Russia who have not bowed the knee to Communism or kissed its image.

It becomes us therefore to be penitent, confident and humbly brave before the mask of terror presented by H-bombs, sputniks and ballistic missiles. We need to make sure that we are morally worthy to be perpetuated as a nation and the God of Sabaoth will guard and protect us. I believe that our country is still the object of God's interest. The warm breath of prayer still hangs as an unseen mist over those woods and templed hills of which we sing, though the praying saints themselves may long since have quitted the land they once loved and baptized with loving tears.

No matter what the circumstances, we Christians should keep our heads. God has not given us the spirit of fear, but of power, of love and of a sound mind. It is a dismal thing to see a son of heaven cringe in terror before the sons of earth. We are taught by the Holy Spirit in Scriptures of truth that fear is a kind of prison for the mind and that by it we may spend a lifetime in bondage.

To recoil from the approach of mental or physical pain is natural, but to allow our minds to become terrorized is quite another thing. The first is a reflex action; the latter is the result of sin and is a work of the devil to bring us into bondage. Terror is or should be foreign to the redeemed mind. True faith delivers from fear by consciously interposing God between it and the object that would make it afraid. The soul that lives in God is surrounded by the divine Presence so that no enemy can approach it without first disposing of God, a palpable impossibility.

I could quote hundreds of passages from the Holy Scriptures to show that God keeps His people and that there is nothing in earth or in hell that can harm a trusting soul. The past is forgiven, the present is in God's keeping and a thousand bright promises give assurance for the future. Yet we are sometimes terrified by the adversary. This is not uncommon but it is unnecessary. We should not try to excuse it, but rather acknowledge it as evidence of our spiritual immaturity.

Through the blood of the everlasting covenant we are as safe here on earth as if we were already in heaven. We have not passed beyond the possibility of physical death, but we have entered a sphere of life where we can afford to die, knowing that for the Christian death is a bright portal to the ineffable glory.

It is entirely possible to reach a place in grace where nothing can panic us. We can have an understanding with God about our yesterdays, our today and our tomorrows. The fear of death and judgment goes out of us as the true fear of God comes in, and that fear has no torment but is rather a light and easy yoke for the soul, one which rests us instead of exhausting us.

Christmas Reformation
Long Overdue

I n these latter-years of the twentieth century no other season of the year reveals so much religion and so little godliness as the Christmas season.

Since Dickens wrote *A Christmas Carol,* scarcely anyone dares to come right out and say what he thinks of Christmas. To do so, we fear, would be to identify ourselves with a nasty old grouch who hated everybody; so we go along with the tinseled festivities, doing our best to preserve a misty smile on our faces and a happy, vibrant ring in our voices, no matter how we feel.

Now, Dickens to the contrary notwithstanding, I do not believe that we are compelled to choose between old Scrooge and Tiny Tim. Surely there is a middle ground where mature, love-inspired,

Spirit-illuminated adults can locate themselves and make up their own minds about that most beautiful but most abused and abased holiday we call Christmas. I for one want to do just that and love everybody in the process.

I never knew an Ebenezer Scrooge. My own childhood was brightened by the annual return of Christmas. My sweet-faced mother struggled to provide a few extras for her family on Christmas morning and somehow she always succeeded. If there was no more than an orange, a popcorn ball and a cheap toy for each of us, it was yet a memorable time for all. Even the old yellow mongrel that lay on the homemade braided rug was on that happy morning treated to a handful of hard candy which he crunched loudly and solemnly to the squealing of delight of the younger children.

The children that later came to my own home could, and I am sure would, testify to the almost unbearable delight Christmas morning brought to them. Their near delirium as they tumbled out of bed and gathered around the tree to unwrap their gifts amid shouts of surprise and delight will never be forgotten by them or by their parents while life and memory endure. No, whoever else might drop in during the day, Scrooge was never there; he'd have died of apoplexy if he had come near the place.

Yet Christmas as it is celebrated today is badly in need of a radical reformation. What was at first a spontaneous expression of an innocent pleasure has been carried to inordinate excess. In one section of Chicago, for instance, the excited citizenry vie with each other each year for the biggest, gaudiest and most vulgar Christmas tree, on the porch, on the lawn, along the street; and one gigantic, flashily dressed and cold but determinedly smiling Santa Claus drives a fully lighted herd of reindeer across the yard and over the house!

How far have we come in the corruption of our tastes from the reverence of the simple shepherds, the chant of the angels and the beauty of the heavenly host! The Star of Bethlehem could not lead a wise man to Christ today; it could not be distinguished amid the millions of artificial lights hung aloft on Main Street by the Merchants Association. No angels could sing loudly enough to make themselves heard above the raucous, ear-splitting rendition of "Silent Night" meant to draw customers to the neighborhood stores.

In our mad materialism we have turned beauty into ashes, prostituted every normal emotion and made merchandise of the holiest gift the world ever knew. Christ came to bring peace and we celebrate His coming by making peace impossible for six weeks of each year. Not peace but tension, fatigue and irritation rule the Christmas season. He came to free us of debt and many respond by going deep into debt each year to buy enervating luxuries for people who do not appreciate them. He came to help the poor and we heap gifts upon those who do not need them. The simple token given out of love has been displaced by expensive presents given because we have been caught in a squeeze and don't know how to back out of it. Not the beauty of the Lord our God is found in such a situation, but the ugliness and deformity of human sin.

Among the harmful abuses of the Christmas season in America is the substitution of Santa Claus for Christ as the chief object of popular interest, especially among the children.

The morality of Mother Goose stories and fairy tales has been questioned by serious-minded Christian parents, but my opinion is that these are relatively harmless because they are told as fiction and the child is fully aware that they are imaginary. With Santa Claus it is not so. The child is taught falsehood as sober truth and is thus grossly deceived during the most sensitive and formative period of his life.

What shall we do? Cultivate humility and frugality. Put the emphasis where the Bible puts it, on the Christ at the right hand of God, not on the babe in the manger. Return to the simplicity that is in Christ. Cleanse our churches of the unscriptural pageantry borrowed from Rome. Take the Scriptures as our guide and refuse to be pressured into conformity to paganism practiced in the name of Christ.

CHAPTER

15

Lift Your Glad Voices

J ust as the book of Psalms is a lyric commentary
on the Old Testament, set to the music of
warm personal devotion, so our great Christian
hymns form a joyous commentary on the New
Testament.

While no instructed Christian would claim for
any hymn the same degree of inspiration that be-
longs to the Psalms, the worshiping singing soul
is easily persuaded that many hymns possess an
inward radiance that is a little more than human.
If not inspired in the full and final sense, they are
yet warm with the breath of the Spirit and sweet
with the fragrance of myrrh and aloes and cassia
out of the ivory palaces.

In the hymns all the basic doctrines of the
Christian faith are celebrated. Were the Scriptures
to be destroyed or made inaccessible to the
Church, it would not be too difficult to extract

from our hymns a complete body of Bible doctrine. This would, of course, lack the authority of the inspired Word, but it might well serve in a dark hour to keep alive the faith of our fathers. As long as the Church can sing her great hymns she cannot be defeated; for hymns are theology set to music.

Hymns do not create truth, nor even reveal it; they celebrate it. They are the response of the trusting heart to a truth revealed or a fact accomplished. God does it and man sings it. God speaks and a hymn is the musical echo of His voice.

No other event in the history of the world has brought forth such a full chorus of song as the resurrection of Christ from the dead. More music has issued from Joseph's empty tomb than from all the concert halls of the world since the dawn of the first civilization. The resurrection was the fact. Hymnody is the response of faith to that fact.

The story of Easter might be told in some fullness of detail by merely stringing together in their proper order lines and verses from our classic hymns. Take for instance the restrained but intensely joyous Latin hymn,

> The strife is o'er, the battle done;
> Now is the Victor's triumph won;
> Now be the song of praise begun—
>   Hallelujah!

There we have pure theology, with an exhortation and an exclamation added. The rest of the hymn develops the doctrine further:

> The powers of death have done their
>   worst,
> But Christ their legion hath dispersed; . . .
> He brake the age-bound chains of hell;
> The bars from heaven's high portals fell.

To each of these couplets is added a joyous call to praise and the ejaculatory Hallelujah! This is hymnody at its best. It does not seek to reveal anything; it assumes that the facts are already known, and sets them forth in a manner that makes praise and song the natural result.

Another Latin hymn dating back to the sixth century begins,

> "Welcome, happy morning!" age to age
>   shall say;
> Hell today is vanquished; Heaven is won
>   today.
> Lo! the Dead is living, God for evermore!
> Him, their true Creator, all His works
>   adore.

This sets forth the theological reason behind the joy of Easter. Christ was dead, but His death was not an accident; neither was it the result of sickness or age. He died to vanquish hell and win heaven for men. Christ was dead, but He is not dead now. Lo! the Dead is living! And how can believing men keep silent?

No Bible-taught Christian can allow himself to live in bondage to days and times and seasons

(Colossians 2:16–17; Romans 14:4–10; 2 Corinthians 3:5–18). He knows he is free from the Law, and the Judaizing brethren who seek to rivet a yoke on his neck will not have much success. But he nevertheless appreciates the value of one day in seven to devote to prayer and praise. And since Christ arose from the dead on the first day, the Bible-loving man will see the spiritual appropriateness of the first day as the Christian's voluntary sabbath day.

In a great and loved hymn by Christopher Wordsworth this idea is set forth with great beauty and unanswerable logic. After praising the first day as a "day of rest and gladness" and a "day of joy and light . . . most beautiful, most bright," he gives three sound reasons for celebrating it:

> On thee, at the creation,
> The light first had its birth;
> On thee, for our salvation,
> Christ rose from depths of earth;
> On thee, our Lord, victorious,
> The Spirit sent from heaven;
> And thus on thee, most glorious,
> A triple light was given.

On the first day light had its birth; on the first day Christ arose; on the first day the Holy Spirit descended. Though there is much other truth to support this, for a true follower of Christ no stronger argument is needed. On the first day he will love to remember Christ's triumph; and each first day will be to him a reminder that Christ rose from depths of earth.

Thank God for the Easter season that serves in some measure to focus the attention of Christians upon that great rock of their historic faith, "Christ is risen!" We can hardly make too much of it. So we shout with the hymnist,

Lift your glad voices in triumph on high,
For Jesus hath risen, and man shall not
    die!

Laboring the Obvious

M any of us who preach the unsearchable riches of Christ are often pretty dull and hard to listen to.

The freshest thought to visit the human mind should be the thought of God. The story of salvation should put a radiancy in the face and a vibrancy in the voice of him that tells it. Yet it is not uncommon to hear the wondrous message given in a manner that makes it difficult for the hearer to concentrate on what is being said. What is wrong?

The conventional answer, "The speaker is not full of the Holy Spirit," does not tell us enough. Many who by every test of life and love are temples of the Spirit manage to sound like a worn-out phonograph record that was not very good in the first place.

It is true that only the Spirit-filled preacher can be morally effective at last; but for the moment we are thinking only of the ability of a speaker to command the attention of his hearers. And if the speaker cannot keep his hearers immediately interested, his message cannot possibly have a long-range effect upon them, no matter how spiritual he may be.

Probably no other part of the Holy Scriptures has suffered as much from dull exposition as have the epistles of Paul. The writings themselves are gems of beauty, lyrical and musical. Sermons based on them should be "as crisp as biting into a fresh apple." Instead they are often as disappointing as biting into a ball of yarn. Why?

It would probably be an oversimplification to name any single cause as being alone responsible for the dullness of our preaching, but I nevertheless venture to suggest that one very important factor is our habit of laboring the obvious. (If any reader should smile and say, "That is what this editorial is doing," I have no defense to offer. At least I see my fault and shall try to remedy it.)

In trying to discover the cause of my aversion to the ministry of certain evangelical Bible teachers I have concluded that it is their incurable habit of laboring the obvious. They seem not to know that elementary truths often repeated dull the spiritual faculties of the saints. Especially is this true when the teacher insists upon playing with theological blocks, spelling out the first principles of the doctrine of Christ apparently with no intention of going on.

The vast majority of our Bible conferences are dedicated to the obvious. Each of the brethren (usually advertised as "widely sought after as a conference speaker") ranges afar throughout the Scriptures to discover additional passages to support truth already known to and believed by 99 percent of his hearers. If the speaker can show that some elementary truth had been hidden in an Old Testament "type" and not before noticed, he is hailed as a profound Bible scholar and eagerly invited back next year.

This engrossment in first principles has an adverse effect upon the evangelical church. It is as if an intelligent child should be forced to stay in the third grade five or six years. The monotony is just too great. The mind cannot remain alert when the elements of surprise and disclosure are missing. Personally I sit through the average orthodox sermon with the same sense of bored frustration one might feel who was reading a mystery story through for the twelfth time.

Our tendency to repeat endlessly a half dozen basic doctrines is the result of our lack of prophetic insight and our failure to meet God in living encounter. The knowledge of God presents a million facets, each one shining with a new ravishing light. The teacher who lives in the heart of God, reads Scriptures with warm devotion, undergoes the discipline and chastisement of the Holy Spirit and presses on toward perfection is sure every now and again to come upon fresh and blessed vistas of truth, old indeed as the Word itself, but bright as the dew on the grass in the morning. The heart that has seen the far glimpses of advanced truth will never be able to keep quiet about them. His experiences will get into his sermons one way or another, and his messages will carry an element of surprise and delight altogether absent from the ordinary Bible talks heard everywhere these days.

Something within the heart of the normal man revolts against motion without progress. Yet this is precisely what we are offered in the vast majority of evangelical churches. Doctrinally these churches are moving around a tight and narrow circle. Their teachers tell them that this circle encompasses all the land of Beulah and warn them of the danger of looking for anything more.

The teaching that consists entirely of reiteration cannot but be dull and wearisome; so the churches try to make up for the religious lassitude they cannot help but feel by introducing extrascriptural diversions and antiscriptural entertainments to provide the stultified saints with a bit of relish for their tedium. It never seems to occur to anyone that there is true joy farther on if they would only escape from the circle and strike out for the hills of God.

To bring news already known; to marshal texts to prove truth everyone believes and no one disputes; to illustrate by endless stories doctrines long familiar; to lay again and again the founda-

tions of repentance from dead works and faith toward God—this is to labor the obvious.

"Therefore leaving the principles of the doctrine of Christ, let us go on unto perfection."

Ability and Responsibility

Ability involves responsibility," wrote the celebrated Dr. Maclaren.

This statement is in complete harmony with the teaching of the Scriptures, yet in our relation to God and our fellow men we are too likely to forget it.

Human beings, as far as they are understanding and just, acknowledge ability as the proper measure of responsibility. The blind man is not held responsible to see nor the deaf man to hear. Even the most oppressive government imposes upon its citizens only such taxes, as it judges him able to pay. To demand more of any man is finally to destroy such ability as he may possess. Any government that would demand more of its citizens than they were able to pay would soon dry up all tribute at its roots and bring upon itself sure destruction.

In an odd but highly significant passage in the Holy Scriptures, we are told that God judges men according to their light.

> And the times of this ignorance God winked at: but now commandeth all men every where to repent: Because he hath appointed a day, in which he will judge the world in righteousness by that man whom he hath ordained; whereof he hath given assurance unto all men, in that he hath raised him from the dead. (Acts 17:30–31)

If as here stated God "overlooked" the times of ignorance before Christ came, is it too much to believe that He may now "overlook" the places where it is not yet known that He came? This is not to imply that God's overlooking men in ancient times absolved them of all responsibility. No, for always there is the light of nature as well as the light of conscience, and these are made effective by "The true light which lighteth every man that cometh into the world" (John 1:9).

Paul cleared this up for us when he wrote, "For as many as have sinned without law shall also perish without law: and as many as have sinned in the law shall be judged by the law" (Romans 2:12). Idolatry is a grave and destructive sin no matter where it is found; but the appearance of Jesus Christ as the Light of the world took away any flimsy excuses men might have had and made them instantly responsible to turn to God from idols. The same holds true wherever the gospel is preached. The heathen are not innocent before they have heard the gospel, but their responsibility is vastly increased after they have heard it.

The principle we are discussing, while it involves responsibility for truth received, goes far beyond this. It involves also our money, our time, our talents and our opportunities.

American economists and politicians these days are talking about our "unprecedented" standard of living, our high income, our push-button conveniences and our huge bank accounts. In spite of the temporary lag in employment this is all true, and to a degree known nowhere else on earth (unless it is in our friendly sister country to the north, which I understand enjoys a prosperity equal to our own).

As sharers in a prosperous economy we Christians must not forget that ability involves responsibility. We have more than our fathers had, and are therefore able to do more for our fellow men than they could do. We are in danger of overlooking this. A larger income may be considered in either of two ways: (1) I earn more; therefore I can spend more and enjoy myself better. (2) I earn more; therefore I am able to do more good for more people and aid in the evangelization of more tribes and nations.

To use increased income to feed the flesh and enjoy greater luxuries is perfectly natural—and that is precisely why it is wrong; it accords with fallen human nature and is of the essence of self-ishness and sin. To accept a larger income as a means whereby we may lay up treasures in heaven accords with the teachings of Christ. Every Christian who has this problem to face should prayerfully consider his larger responsibility in the light of his increased ability.

A word must be added also concerning those abilities we call time, talents and opportunities. These are not equal among all Christians, and a moment of sanctified thinking would lead us to conclude that God's requirements are not the same for all. From the largest sheep the shepherd expects the most wool, and from the largest tree we expect the most fruit.

The rule for individual responsibility was laid down by Peter. "If any man speak, let him speak as the oracles of God; if any man minister, let him do it as of the ability which God giveth" (1 Peter 4:11). With this agree the words of Paul:

> For I say, through the grace given unto me, to every man that is among you, not to think of himself more highly than he ought to think; but to think soberly, according as God hath dealt to every man the measure of faith. (Romans 12:3)

Some Christians die young; others linger on and, like tall candles, burn down to the socket. The first have had less of the ability called time, and for that reason their responsibility will not be so great.

The size of a man's mind, the opportunities he enjoys and the talents he has received determine his responsibility to God and his fellow men. While the size and the amount of fruit a life bears will vary with the individual, the quality is expected to be equal with all. To be holy is the duty and privilege of every true Christian. Ability is something else and the two should never be confused.

Beware the Romantic
Spirit in Religion

Most persons are, I suppose, more or less romantic in one proper meaning of that word, and my observation leads me to conclude that religious persons are likely to become more than ordinarily so.

Of course it is not the religious man's attitude toward the opposite sex that I have in mind here, but his attitude toward all of life. And if anyone should doubt that anything as excellent as religion could cause an excess of anything as questionable as the romantic spirit, I answer that every good thing has its hazards and that the best things may lead to the worst if allowed to run wild, unexamined and undirected.

The romantic habit of mind in religion is easy to identify. The romantic religionist thinks with his nerve ends, substitutes words for deeds, accepts the unreal with misty-eyed credulity, confuses wishing with believing and thinks that if a man feels virtuous he is so in fact.

The comfortable drone of the Gloria Patri or the Lord's Prayer repeated in unison has a marvelously tranquilizing effect upon such a man. He may sleep through the sermon, or if he remains alert enough to hear it he will never apply it to his own life in a practical way; yet the sonorous sound of the benediction followed by the sweet choral response gives him the feeling that he has profited immeasurably by his attendance at church. On the way out he will smile, shake hands, congratulate the preacher and go his way completely unchanged. Tomorrow he will drive just as hard a bargain in his business, tell the same shady stories, cheat on his income tax, shout at the driver ahead of him, bark at his wife, overeat and otherwise live like the son of this world that he in fact is.

The next Sunday he will go to church again and for a few moments experience the same radiant feeling of well-being and good will toward men that he has enjoyed once a week for years. He simply cannot relate religion to life. To him Christianity has no necessary bearing upon present conduct. It is only a pleasant thing like, say, a sunset or a Swedish massage, and it is nothing more.

The romantic attitude was not unknown in Bible times. The apostle John warned against one of its manifestations when he wrote, "My little children, let us not love in word, neither in tongue, but in deed and in truth. And by this we know that we are of the truth, and shall assure our hearts before him" (1 John 3:18–19). Kierkegaard wisely said that there is nothing in the Holy Scriptures about loving man in the mass, only about loving our neighbor as ourself. Yet there is among us much evidence of love for mankind and little evidence of love for the individual. The idea of love for our brother is a beautiful thing as long as it does not demand that we put it into practice on some particular person; then it becomes a nuisance.

Many Christians love foreign missions who cannot bring themselves to love foreigners. They pray tenderly for the colored man in Africa but they cannot stand him in America. They love the Chinese in Hong Kong and are willing to give generously to send someone to convert him, but they never try to convert him when he is in a laundry on Main Street. They wear a flower to honor mother on her day, but she is too much of an inconvenience to be welcome in the home, so she is shunted from place to place till she is so sick and weary that she can be sent at last to a nursing home to await the end.

I am well aware that this kind of thinking is branded as "negative" or "cynical" and that most Christians are not willing to face up to it. It was so also in the time of Christ's earthly ministry. Israel wallowed in unreality. The lives of the priests and people did not support their words. They talked a good life and lived a bad one. Our Lord could not abide the artificial and the unreal. Pretense was offensive to Him wherever He found it and He said so plainly. The consequence of His plain talk is known to the ages.

I believe that there are a few Christians even in these degenerate days who want reality more than they want consolation and who would rather hear disturbing truth than comforting error. They want to know exactly where they stand now while they can do something about it. They are willing to believe the worst about themselves and the best about the saving power of Christ. These do not need to take refuge in fancy. They will soon find reality.

Joy Will Come in
Its Own Time

We can know our present properly only as we know our past, and in that past there occurred something disgraceful and tragic, namely, the loss of our moral character and rebellion against our Creator. That we also lost our happiness is of secondary importance since it is but a result of our alienation from God and not a part of that alienation.

The primary work of Christ in redemption is to justify, sanctify and ultimately to glorify a company of persons salvaged from the ruin of the human race.

For the convenience of any who may not be familiar with the words used here I would explain that *justify* means to declare righteous before God, *sanctify* means to make holy, and *glorify* means in effect to remake the entire personality after the image of Christ. This will fit us to dwell eternally in that heaven about which the Bible speaks and which is both a state of being and a location. In that heaven the ransomed will experience unclouded communion with the Triune God; and that will itself assure unalloyed blessedness.

I have just now used the word "ruin" and associated it with the human race. This is not a figure of speech nor is it an extravagant or irresponsible use of a word. The race lies in ruin, spiritually, morally and physically. History and the daily newspaper testify to our moral ruin. The long parade of gods both virtuous and obscene and a thousand varieties of vain and meaningless religious practices declare our spiritual degeneration, while disease, old age and death testify sadly to the completeness of our physical decay.

We inhabit a world suspended halfway between heaven and hell, alienated from one and not yet abandoned to the other. By nature we are unholy and by practice unrighteous. That we are unhappy, I repeat, is of small consequence. Our first and imperative duty is to escape the corruption which is in the world as Lot escaped the moral ruin of Sodom. It is of overwhelming importance to us that we should seek the favor of God while it is possible to find it and that we should bring ourselves under the plenary authority of Jesus Christ in complete and voluntary obedience. To do this is to invite trouble from a hostile world and to incur such unhappiness as may naturally follow. Add to this the temptations of the devil and a lifelong struggle with the flesh and it will be obvious that we will need to defer most of our enjoyments to a more appropriate time.

Against this background of fact our childish desire to be happy is seen to be a morally ugly thing, wholly foreign to the Spirit of the Man of Sorrows and contrary to the teaching and practice of His apostles.

Any appeal to the public in the name of Christ that rises no higher than an invitation to tranquillity must be recognized as mere humanism with a few words of Jesus thrown in to make it appear Christian. But only that is truly Christian which accords with the Spirit and teachings of Christ. Everything else is un-Christian or anti-Christian, no matter whence it emanates.

Strange, is it not, that we dare without shame to alter, to modulate the words of Christ while speaking for Christ to the very ones for whom He died?

Christ calls men to carry a cross; we call them to have fun in His Name. He calls them to forsake the world; we assure them that if they but accept Jesus the world is their oyster. He calls them to suffer; we call them to enjoy all the bourgeois comforts modern civilization affords. He calls them to self-abnegation and death. We call them to spread themselves like green bay trees or perchance even to become stars in a pitiful fifth-rate religious zodiac. He calls them to holiness; we call them to a cheap and tawdry happiness that would have been rejected with scorn by the least of the Stoic philosophers.

In a world like this, with conditions being what they are, what should a serious-minded Christian do? The answer is easy to give but hard to follow.

First, accept the truth concerning yourself. You do not go to a doctor to seek consolation but to find out what is wrong and what to do about it. Seek the kingdom of God and His righteousness. Seek through Jesus Christ a right relationship to your fellow man. Set about reverently to amend your doings. Magnify God, mortify the flesh, simplify your life. Take up your cross and learn of Jesus Christ to die to this world that He may raise you up in due time.

If you will do these things in faith and love, you will know peace, but it will be the peace of God that passes all understanding. You will know joy, but it will be the joy of resurrection, not the irresponsible happiness of men who insist on carnal enjoyments. You will know the comfort of the indwelling Spirit which will often spring up like a well of water in the desert, not because you have sought it but have sought rather to do the will of God at any price.

As I have said before, we can afford to suffer now; we'll have a long eternity to enjoy ourselves. And our enjoyment will be valid and pure, for it will come in the right way at the right time.

Temperance, the Rare Virtue

W ere I to select a word which I felt best described the modern American temper that word would be excess.

Almost everything we do, we overdo. We are forever creating monstrosities. If it moves, it moves too fast; if it is high, it is too high; if it makes noise, the noise is ridiculously loud; if we make a car, it is sure to be grotesquely large and gaudy with vastly more power than is required for the transportation we desire. We have too many telephones, too many filling stations, too many stores. Our national debt is astronomical, our waste incredible; our highways are too many, too complex and too expensive. Vacations are too long and too strenuous. Our swapping of Christmas gifts has become an irksome rat race not remotely related to the blessed Advent. Music we hear everywhere till our ears are suffocated in a welter of inappropriate melody.

In an effort to manage and direct the enormous energies, the prodigious activities and the fabulous wealth of our people, bureau has followed bureau and agency has sprung up on agency till bureau and agency are getting completely out of hand and are themselves becoming huge, back-breaking burdens that constitute a serious threat to the health of the national body.

Without doubt we are out of control and it may be that we have reached the point of no return. We may never recover from our mighty binge. It should be said, however, that if we alone are destroying ourselves by excess, it is because we are the only nation rich enough to do it successfully and to get such a whale of a lot of pleasure out of the job. Others have blown their brains out, but we can afford to blow the whole head off as well, and many of the nations that gaze on us with self-righteous horror are merely jealous of us. They would do the same thing if they had the money. We are all alike after all.

Well, all that I have said so far is but a circumlocutory way of getting at a well-known truth: that when mankind fell one effect of the fall was the loss of control. Those divinely implanted powers within him got out of hand and turned from their normal uses to become servants of the flesh and the devil.

It has been obvious to me that almost every sin is but a natural good perverted or carried to excess. Self-respect is turned into pride; natural appetite becomes gluttony; sleep goes on to become sloth; sex goes awry and turns to sodomy; love degenerates into lechery; praise sinks to flattery; determination hardens into obstinacy; a natural childish love of play grows up with the man and becomes a multi-billion dollar business wherein tens of thousands of able-bodied persons waste their lives playing for the amusement of the millions of bored adults who are more than willing to work hard to obtain money to watch them play.

Except for the fact that anything is as easy for God as anything else, it would be proper to say that in His work of saving men God took upon Himself a herculean undertaking. From our low viewpoint it would appear much easier to create the human race than to recreate it; it would seem far less difficult to make a man in the divine image than to remake him in that image after he had been stamped with the likeness of sin. But since God has all the power there is to achieve the purposes conceived by all the wisdom there is, we may relieve ourselves of any anxiety. The zeal of the Lord of hosts will perform this.

The problem God faced in redemption is manyfold. How to square the moral account so that God might be just and the Justifier of them that believe; how to reconcile man to Himself; how to recreate a human spirit while allowing all the essential qualities to remain; how to indwell a personality without displacing it; how to work in the believing man's heart, turn it toward righteousness and still leave free the human will—these are some of the problems, to us impossible but to God not only possible but effortlessly easy.

The question of control enters here, for if the work of redemption is to be complete our basic propensity toward perversion and excess must be reversed. All our powers must be sanctified and brought under the direction of the Spirit. From His throne in the believer's heart Christ must reign over the entire kingdom of Mansoul with all its precincts and provinces. The age-old curse of inordinateness and excess must be destroyed.

For this reason the beautiful word temperance occurs strategically in the theology of the New Testament. Temperance is the helmsman in easy control of the powerful ship as it ploughs through the sea with all parts working in harmony. Temperance is that in the Christian man's life which brings every faculty into harmony with every other, and the total personality into accord with God's plan for the whole man. In a life so directed there can be no place for excess.

Two things need to be added. One is that temperance is not automatic. It is listed among the fruit of the Spirit, but it requires prayer, Bible reading, cross-bearing, hard discipline, obedience and self-denial before it can become a fixed part of the Christian's character.

The second is that a man or woman in Christ who has achieved true self-control may expect to be very much out of step with the world. Human beings given to excess will not take kindly to the

Spirit-filled, temperate soul living among them. After he is dead they may build his sepulchre or name a college after him, but that will be a bit late for his comfort. He had a tough time of it while he lived.

21

The Dangers of
Overstimulation

It is common knowledge that life proceeds by the simple interplay of stimulation and response. Light stimulates the eye to see, sound waves stimulate the ear to hear, food stimulates the digestive processes, and so throughout the entire body.

Our emotions also require stimulation to trigger them off. The crying of a child in pain, for instance, may arouse uncontrollable feelings of pity in the heart of the mother and prod her to swift, tender ministrations to relieve the child.

The whole human personality, physical, mental and spiritual, tends to remain quiescent until appropriate stimuli arouse it to action. That is the way God made us, and as long as everything is kept in proper balance our lives go on their normal way.

Stimulation is good; overstimulation is a positive evil productive of every kind of physical and mental injury. And overstimulation has in recent years become a recognized part of our civilization. Indeed it is now a *necessary* part of it. The modern edifice we call our way of life would collapse were it not upheld by the pressure of abnormal stimulation.

The beating heart of our economy is the production and sale of consumer goods. The average person is likely to be a sluggish buyer unless he is needled into buying by high-pressure advertising. Hence the vast amounts spent each year and the tricky methods employed to persuade the public to buy. I think we have reached a place in the United States where the country must be overstimulated to prevent a serious depression. Take the pressure off and sales would probably decline sufficiently to throw the national economy into chaos.

Is overstimulation, then, a good thing for the country? Only in the same way that dope is good for the confirmed addict or another shot of liquor is good for the alcoholic. Which is to say that it is not good at all, but merely necessary because of the unhealthy condition of the patient.

The tendency toward excessive stimulation is seen everywhere. Entertainment that once satisfied people now excites nothing more enjoyable than boredom. The theatrical pages of the daily papers tingle with such words as "tantalizing," "suspenseful," "breathless," "terrifying," "explosive." Recently one particularly spine-chilling number at the local bijou advertised itself as "the world's greatest horrorama" and promised that the jaded citizens who came to see it would find it "a billion-shock monsterpiece."

This kind of thing in varying degree is found also in our automobiles, furniture, books, art, music, clothes, and gives evidence of mass emotional dope addiction in an advanced stage. People have lost the ability to loaf and think and invite their souls. They must be constantly excited by external agents to make life bearable for them. It would be interesting and probably depressing to know how many American housewives each day throb and quiver to the synthetic joys and sorrows of fictional radio and TV characters with whom they have come to identify themselves emotionally almost as closely as with members of their own families.

My words are addressed to regenerated souls who are humble enough to be willing to learn and hungry enough to want to. I have not the dimmest hope that any politician, economist or advertiser will heed my warning even if what I write should by accident fall into his hands. The inhabitants of Vanity Fair are not likely to listen to the words of a Christian. They are under the control of "the carnal mind [which] is enmity against God: for it is not subject to the law of God, neither indeed can be" (Romans 8:7).

But the Christian needs stimulation. This the Bible teaches with great plainness and candor as in such passages as these: "Wherefore I put thee in re-membrance that thou stir up the gift of God, which is in thee by the putting on of my hands" (1 Timothy 1:6). "Exhort one another daily" (Hebrews 3:13). Every call to repentance, every exhortation to advance in the spiritual life, is meant to arouse the sluggish heart to seek God and His righteousness. Christ Himself was "moved with compassion" when He saw the hungry multitudes. Paul's Macedonian vision was given to stimulate missionary action. The so-called hortatory passages in the New Testament are there to inspire moral obedience.

Overstimulation, however, is always bad. Certain highly emotional religious groups appear entirely incapable of carrying on unless they are aroused to a high pitch of nervous excitement which, incidentally, they mistake for the movings of the Holy Spirit. Serious as this is I still believe it is more sincere and less injurious than that new playboy type of Fundamentalism which can only exist by high voltage external stimuli. One such group recently advertised a missionary rally as a "missionary spectacular." These misguided friends simply do not see the glaring inconsistency between this and legitimate New Testament methods.

No Christian should need any other stimulation than that afforded by the Word of God, the indwelling Holy Spirit and prayer. These along with the overwhelming needs of the lost world should provide all normal stimulation. Anything beyond this is unnecessary and can be dangerous.

The Meaning of Christmas

Everywhere, everywhere, Christmas to-night!"—Phillips Brooks.

That there were in the world multiplied millions who had never heard of Christmas did not matter to our poet for the purpose of his poem. He was expressing an emotional fact, not a statistical one.

Throughout the Western world we tend to follow the poet and approach Christmas emotionally instead of factually. It is the romance of Christmas that gives it its extraordinary appeal to that relatively small number of persons of the earth's population who regularly celebrate it.

So completely are we carried away by the excitement of this midwinter festival that we are apt to forget that its romantic appeal is the least significant thing about it. The theology of Christmas too easily gets lost under the gay wrappings, yet apart from its theological meaning it really has none at all. A half dozen doctrinally sound carols serve to keep alive the great deep truth of the Incarnation, but aside from these, popular Christmas music is void of any real lasting truth. The English mouse that was not even stirring, the German Tannenbaum so fair and lovely and the American red-nosed reindeer that has nothing to recommend it have pretty well taken over in Christmas poetry and song. These along with merry old St. Nicholas have about displaced Christian theology.

We must not forget that the Church is the custodian of a truth so grave and urgent that its importance can not be overemphasized, and so vast and incomprehensible that even an apostle did not try to explain it; rather it burst forth from him as an astonished exclamation:

> And without controversy great is the mystery of godliness: God was manifest in the flesh, justified in the Spirit, seen of angels, preached unto the Gentiles, believed on in the world, received up into glory. (1 Timothy 3:16)

This is what the Church is trying to say to mankind but her voice these days is thin and weak and scarcely heard amid the commercialized clangor of "Silent Night."

It does seem strange that so many persons become excited about Christmas and so few stop to inquire into its meaning; but I suppose this odd phenomenon is quite in harmony with our unfortunate human habit of magnifying trivialities and ignoring matters of greatest import. The same man who will check his tires and consult his road map with utmost care before starting on a journey may travel for a lifetime on the way that knows no return and never once pause to ask whether or not he is headed in the right direction.

The Christmas message, when stripped of its pagan overtones, is relatively simple: God is come to earth in the form of man. Around this one dogma the whole question of meaning revolves. God did come or He did not; He is come or He is not, and the vast accumulation of sentimental notions and romantic practices that go to make up our modern Christmas cannot give evidence on one side or the other.

Certain religious teachers in apostolic times refused to believe that Jesus was actually God come in the flesh. They were willing to exhaust the language of unctuous flattery to describe His glorious manhood, but they would have none of His deity. Their basic philosophy forbade them to believe that there could ever be a union of God and human flesh. Matter, they said, is essentially evil. God who is impeccably holy could never allow Himself contact with evil. Human flesh is matter, therefore God is not come in the flesh.

Certainly it would not be difficult to refute this negative teaching. One would only need to demonstrate the error of the major premise, the essential sinfulness of matter, and the whole thing would collapse. But that would be to match reason against reason and take the mystery of godliness out of the realm of faith and make of it merely another religious philosophy. Then we would have rationalism with a thin Christian veneer. How long before the veneer wore off and we had only rationalism?

While faith contains an element of reason, it is essentially moral rather than intellectual. In the New Testament unbelief is a sin, and this could not be so if belief were no more than a verdict based upon evidence. There is nothing unreasonable about the Christian message, but its appeal is not primarily to reason. At a specific time in a certain place God became flesh, but the transcendence of Christ over the human conscience is not historic; it is intimate, direct and personal.

Christ's coming to Bethlehem's manger was in harmony with the primary fact of His secret presence in the world in preincarnate times as the Light that lighteth every man. The sum of the New Testament teaching about this is that Christ's claims are self-validating and will be rejected only by those who love evil. Whenever Christ is preached in the power of the Spirit, a judgment seat is erected and each hearer stands to be judged by his response to the message. His moral responsibility is not to a lesson in religious history but to the divine Person who now confronts him.

"Everywhere, everywhere, Christmas tonight." But Christmas either means more than is popularly supposed or it means nothing. We had better decide.

CHAPTER

23

A Glance Back
and a Look Forward

A popular French writer once suggested that it takes intellectual powers approaching genius to escape from the illusion of anniversaries.

Not possessing such powers I can only look wistfully at the mental giant who dwells in such timeless tranquillity and make what terms I can with the circling of the spheres. I know well enough that at midnight, December 31, nothing unusual will actually happen except in my head and the heads of others like me. I will *think* a new year that is new only because men have arbitrarily called it so, and feel myself passing over a line that is not really there. The whole thing will be imaginary and yet I cannot quite escape the fascination of it.

The Jews start the New Year on one date, and the Christians on another, and we cannot forget that the calendar has been pushed around quite a bit since men began to count time by years. Still the observation of the New Year is useful if it persuades us to slow down and let our souls catch up. And I think that is the real value of watch night services. We might do the same thing any night, but it is not likely that we will, so we may profit by taking advantage of the New Year service to examine our lives and ask of God strength to do better in the future than we have done in the past.

While the backward look should be searching and realistic, it should also be brief, for as a Black minister said in my hearing recently, "It's difficult to climb a mountain looking back." A quick glance over our shoulder is good, for it will sober us and remind us that we must some day give an account of the deeds done in the body.

For some of us last year was one in which we did not acquit ourselves very nobly as Christians, considering the infinite power available to us through the indwelling Spirit. But through the goodness of God we may go to the school of our failures. The man of illuminated mind will learn from his mistakes, yes even from his sins. If his heart is trusting and penitent, he can be a better man next year for last year's fault—but let him not return again to folly. Repentance should be radical and thorough, and the best repentance for a wrong act, as Fenelon said, is not to do it again. Charles Wesley called Pharaoh "a penitent in vain" because he repented under the pressure of each plague and went back to sinning as soon as the plague was removed.

In seeking to evaluate our conduct over the past year, we must be careful to avoid two opposite errors: the first is being too easy on ourselves and the second is being too hard.

Contrary to what we hear constantly, especially from certain enthusiastic brethren determinedly bent on revival according to their particular idea of it, we do not always do God service by scourging ourselves. The evangelical flagellant who thinks to please God by punishing himself is as far from the truth, though in the other direction, as the rabbi who in all seriousness declared, "If there are two righteous men in the world they are myself and my son; if one, it is myself."

To demand too much of ourselves is to admit tacitly that we have at least some degree of confidence in our native moral ability, and of course it is also to admit that our confidence in God is correspondingly weak. The man who knows himself deeply will not expect anything of himself and will not be disappointed when he fails to produce.

Brother Lawrence expressed the highest moral wisdom when he testified that if he stumbled and fell he turned at once to God and said, "O Lord, this is what You may expect of me if You leave me to myself." He then accepted forgiveness, thanked God and gave himself no further concern about the matter. Meister Eckhart said that when we rise above sin and turn away from it, God will act as if we had never sinned at all and will never let our past sins count against us, for He is a God of the present and takes a man as He finds him without regard to his past. Of course this all presupposes true repentance and faith and is written not to minimize sin but to magnify grace.

So much for last year; but what about the year ahead? Well, there are said to be three thousand promises in the Holy Scriptures and they are all ours if we know what to do with them. For the Christian there is no unexplored territory. "When he putteth forth his own sheep, he goeth before them." The footprint of the obedient sheep is always found within the larger footprint of the Shepherd.

It is wholly impossible for us to know what lies before us, but it is possible to know something vastly more important. A quaint but godly American preacher of a generation past said it for us. "Abraham went out not knowing whither he went," said he, "but he knew Who was going with him." We cannot know for certain the what and the whither of our earthly pilgrimage, but we can be sure of the Who. And nothing else really matters.

Singing Commentary

A commentary, as everyone knows, is a book written by a commentator, and a commentator is one who comments on what God has said, hoping thereby to make us understand what God meant.

The commentary may be good if we know how to use it, harmful if we do not. Its usefulness lies in this, that it provides background material which the average Christian is not able to gather for himself and thus often proves a real aid in the study of the Bible.

But it is not an unmixed blessing. It has at least three serious weaknesses. One is that it soon becomes known as an "authority." Let a man be quoted often enough and be dead long enough and he is likely to be canonized by his grateful readers and his writings given oracular standing before the Christian public. The pronouncement of a revered commentator often exercises over the mind of a Protestant a sway as tyrannical as that of a papal bull over the conscience of a Catholic.

Another disadvantage of a commentary is that it tends to destroy the art of meditation. We find it easier to turn to the commentary than to brood long and lovingly over a difficult passage, waiting for the light to break. This habit of taking the quick and painless way to knowledge is particularly bad for the minister, for it often sends him into the pulpit with borrowed armor. Even if what he learned is true, he got it by consultation instead of by meditation and the quality is sure to be impaired.

A third weakness of the commentary, or at least of the commentary habit, is that it makes for a uniformity of belief not only on major theological tenets, which is desirable, but on minor ones, which is not. Let a hundred preachers lean on Matthew Henry or Adam Clarke. Then let each preacher be heard by five hundred parishioners each Sunday for a year. Result: You have thousands of Christians accepting as divine truth the religious opinions of two good and wise men, opinions which may in the first place have been nothing more than educated guesses. And yet, in spite of these drawbacks, a commentary is a good and useful tool for any Christian to own.

The standard commentaries for the most part, however, make rather heavy reading. They almost always walk and if occasionally they run, they never run fast or far, and they rarely mount up with wings as eagles. For this reason I turn frequently with considerable pleasure to Charles Wesley's poetic commentary, a modest work of only 1,100 pages, printed in London in the last decade of the eighteenth century.

Wesley admits that many of his thoughts are gleaned from others, but a deep reverence permeates the whole, and a glowing love for God and the inspired Word breathes on every page. It is possible in such a small work to touch only the shining peaks of truth, so the commentary is far from complete; but often the hymnist puts into a single stanza a happy comment which, if not so informative, is highly stimulating to the religious imagination. I offer here a few examples taken from the section on the Book of Exodus.

When God told Moses to go unto Pharaoh and demand the release of Israel, Moses pleaded, "O my Lord, I am not eloquent" (Exodus 4:10). Here is a dry comment by Wesley,

> How ready is the man to go
>   Whom God hath never sent—
> How timorous, diffident and slow
>   His chosen instrument!

On the knotty problem of God hardening Pharaoh's heart Wesley offers this interpretation,

> There needed, Lord, no act of Thine,
> If Pharaoh had a heart like mine:
> One moment leave me but alone,
> And mine alas is turned to stone!

Hundreds of pages of labored prose have been written about this matter that did not say as much or say it as well.

Wesley believed in the freedom of the will, but he saw also the necessity of a prevenient working of divine grace in the heart before the lost man can repent. In a manner characteristic of him he transferred the impenitence of Pharaoh to himself:

> Such is the stubbornness of man!
>   So deep in me the evil lies!
> Chastised a thousand times in vain,
>   I still against Thy judgments rise;
>
> Not all Thy judgments can convert
>   This sinner, or this sin remove,
> Unless Thou find it in Thy heart
>   To soften mine by pardoning love.

How easy it is to read the dramatic story of the Exodus without profit; but in Wesley's musical commentary everything that happened there has a meaning for the Christian. For instance, the whole matter of God turning Egypt's water into blood ceases to be a problem to cloud the mind and becomes sunshine for the heart. The words "The waters . . . were turned to blood" get this happy comment,

> He turned their water into blood,
>   When vengeance was His dread
>   design:
> But thanks to the incarnate God,
>   He turned our water into wine!

Our Imperfect View of Truth

The soul of man, says Matthew Arnold, is a mirror suspended on a cord, turning in every breeze, always reflecting what is before it but never reflecting more than a small part of the whole.

The size of the mirror varies from man to man, but no one is able to comprehend the vast panorama that lies before and around us. The mental giant has a larger mirror, to be sure, but even the largest is pathetically small.

As long as we know that our view of truth is partial we can preserve that humbleness of mind appropriate to the circumstances; but let us once get the notion that our view is total and we become intellectually intolerant. Let us become convinced that ours is the only sensible view and our ability to learn dies instantly.

None of us should imagine that he has a perfect view of truth. The eye that can see all truth at once without distortion is surely not to be found in this world of fallen men; indeed there may be reason to question whether such an eye exists even among the saints above. Whether such perfection will be granted the redeemed in the glorified state is also doubtful, though Paul's words, "Now I know in part; but then shall I know even as also I am known," give us reason to believe that at the redemption of the body our knowledge will be vastly increased. That this cannot mean absolute knowledge, however, is clear. There can be only one Absolute. Infinitude is an attribute God cannot share with His creatures. To "know as we are known" probably means not "as fully as we are known" but rather "know by direct experience."

Someone has advanced the theory that religious denominations result from differences of temperament among those who compose the larger body of Christians; that new believers tend to seek the fellowship of those whose peculiar beliefs and emphases create a climate most agreeable to their own temperament.

This is an interesting hypothesis but hardly accounts for all the facts. A denomination is but "the lengthened shadow of a man," and the man whose shadow it is must have had powerful convictions concerning certain particular truths or he would not have founded the denomination in the first place. Those who are born into the denomination adopt its views without realizing that there are any others. The religious maverick who (as this writer) was converted to Christ out of a nonreligious home without denominational preference or prejudice is likely to attach himself to the first and nearest Christian fellowship that offers itself.

The new convert is sure to feel the need of instruction and will drink up whatever he hears from the pulpit, accepting not only the doctrines but the emphases as well. Soon he will speak the language of his group and will speak it with their accent. Then he will judge the spirituality and orthodoxy of all other Christians as much by the accent as by the language itself.

Unfortunately indoctrination of a new Christian often means no more than giving him a thorough course in partial truth with the tacit understanding that this is all there is. I am sure we do not mean to do this, but it is what too often happens nevertheless. Of course narrowness, intolerance and bigotry result from this as certainly as an oak from an acorn.

I have seen the motto, "In essentials unity; in nonessentials charity," and I have looked for its incarnation in men and churches without finding it, one reason being that Christians cannot agree on what is and what is not essential. Each one believes that his fragment of truth is essential and his neighbor's unessential, and that brings us right back where we started.

Unity among Christians will not, in my opinion, be achieved short of the Second Advent. There are too many factors working against it.

But a greater degree of unity might be realized if we all approached the truth with deeper humility. No one knows everything, not saint nor scholar nor reformer nor theologian. Even Solomon in all his glory must have overlooked something.

It might help us also to remember that truth occurs both in the singular and in the plural. There are within the Holy Scriptures truth and truths, all inspired and all profitable, but certainly not all equally clear. Great and good men have differed about the meaning of certain texts, but all served their generation by the will of God and fell on sleep. Christ said not, "I am the truths," but "I am the Truth." He gathers up in Himself all truth and truths. To know Him is to know the Truth in living experience, but it is not to know all truths in intellectual apprehension. Let us be careful lest we see a truth in the Word and mistake it for the Truth. There is a mighty difference.

It has always been a source of great delight to me to discover the hymns of the Calvinists Watts, Newton and Cowper in the hymnbook edited by John Wesley, the Arminian. And not a few of the Wesleyan hymns are bound up with the hymns of Isaac Watts published as long ago as 1823.

When Wesley was dying, so we are told, he tried to sing, though his voice was all but gone from him. Someone stooped low over his bed and heard coming from his lips the whispered words of Watts' hymn,

I'll praise my Maker while I've breath,
And when my voice is lost in death,
Praise shall employ my nobler powers; . . .

Fine points of theology are not important at such a time.

The Easter Emphasis

At the risk of sounding more than slightly repetitious, I want to urge again that we Christians look to our doctrinal emphases.

If we would know the power of truth we must emphasize it. Creedal truth is coal lying inert in the depths of the earth waiting release. Dig it out, shovel it into the combustion chamber of some huge engine, and the mighty energy that lay asleep for centuries will create light and heat and cause the machinery of a great factory to surge into productive action. The theory of coal never turned a wheel nor warmed a hearth. Power must be released to be made effective.

In the redemptive work of Christ three major epochs may be noted: His birth, His death and His subsequent elevation to the right hand of God. These are the three main pillars that uphold the temple of Christianity; upon them rest all the hopes of mankind, world without end. All else that He did takes its meaning from these three Godlike deeds.

It is imperative that we believe all these truths, but the big question is where to lay the emphasis. Which truth should, at a given time, receive the sharpest accent? We are exhorted to look unto Jesus, but where shall we look? Unto Jesus in the manger? on the cross? at the throne? These questions are far from academic. It is of great practical importance to us that we get the right answer.

Of course we must include in our total creed the manger, the cross and the throne. All that is symbolized by these three objects must be present to the gaze of faith; all is necessary to a proper understanding of the Christian evangel. No single tenet of our creed must be abandoned or even relaxed, for each is joined to the other by a living bond. But while all truth is to be at all times to be held inviolate, not every truth is to be at all times emphasized equally with every other. Our Lord indicated as much when He spoke of the faithful and wise steward who gave to his master's household "their portion of meat in due season" (Luke 12:42b).

Mary brought forth her firstborn Son and wrapped Him in swaddling clothes and laid Him in a manger. Wise men came to worship, shepherds wondered and angels chanted of peace and good will towards men. All taken together this scene is so chastely beautiful, so winsome, so tender, that the like of it is not found anywhere in the literature of the world. It is not hard to see why Christians have tended to place such emphasis upon the manger, the meek-eyed virgin and the Christ child. In certain Christian circles the major emphasis is made to fall upon the child in the manger. Why this is so is understandable, but the emphasis is nevertheless misplaced.

Christ was born that He might become a man and became a man that He might give His life a ransom for many. Neither the birth nor the dying were ends in themselves. As He was born to die, so did He die that He might atone, and rise that He might justify freely all who take refuge in Him. His birth and His death are history. His appearance at the mercy seat is not history past, but a present, continuing fact, to the instructed Christian the most glorious fact his trusting heart can entertain.

This Easter season might be a good time to get our emphases corrected. Let us remember that weakness lies at the manger, death at the cross and power at the throne. Our Christ is not in a manger. Indeed, New Testament theology nowhere presents the Christ child as an object of saving faith. The gospel that stops at the manger is another gospel and no good news at all. The church that still gathers around the manger can only be weak and misty-eyed, mistaking sentimentality for the power of the Holy Spirit.

As there is now no babe in the manger at Bethlehem so there is no man on the cross at Jerusalem. To worship the babe in the manger or the man on the cross is to reverse the redemptive processes of God and turn the clock back on His eternal purposes. Let the church place its major emphasis upon the cross and there can be only pessimism, gloom and fruitless remorse. Let a sick man die hugging a crucifix and what have we there? Two dead men in a bed, neither of which can help the other.

The glory of the Christian faith is that the Christ who died for our sins rose again for our justification. We should joyfully remember His birth and gratefully muse on His dying, but the crown of all our hopes is with Him at the Father's right hand.

Paul gloried in the cross and refused to preach anything except Christ and Him crucified, but to him the cross stood for the whole redemptive work of Christ. In his epistles Paul writes of the incarnation and the crucifixion, yet he stops not at the manger or the cross but constantly sweeps our thoughts on to the resurrection and upward to the ascension and the throne.

"All power is given unto me in heaven and in earth" (Matthew 28:18), said our risen Lord before He went up on high, and the first Christians believed Him and went forth to share His triumph. "With great power gave the apostles witness of the resurrection of the Lord Jesus: and great grace was upon them all" (Acts 4:33).

Should the Church shift her emphasis from the weakness of the manger and the death of the cross to the life and power of the enthroned Christ, perhaps she might recapture her lost glory. It is worth a try.

The Teachings of Christ
Are for Christians

The talk is now that if the world is to escape near or total annihilation it must turn for help to the ethics of Jesus. The argument runs something like this:

Within the last century man has leaped ahead in scientific achievement but has lagged far behind morally, with the result that he is now technically capable of destroying the world and morally incapable of restraining himself from doing so. Unless the nations of the earth become imbued with the spirit of peace and good will it is highly probable that some trigger-happy politician will fire his shiny new rifle into the ammunition dump and blow up the world.

Because the dump is stored with nuclear explosives any chance humans who escape the big blow will go out to propagate a race of subhuman mutants, hairless, toothless and deformed. The boys who draw the horror comics enable us to visualize those tragic victims of strontium-90 centuries hence clawing through the twisted rubble of what was once New York or London, emitting simian grunts, wholly unaware of the meaning of the bits of history they pick up and toss impatiently away.

No one with a trace of human pity can think of the effects of nuclear warfare without feeling utter abhorrence for such a thing and deepest compassion for those who may sometime be caught in its fiery hell. In it man's age-old inhumanity to man will have through the ingenuity of modern science surely reached the peak of all possible frightfulness.

Yet we Christians would be foolish to allow ourselves to be carried away by the ominous predictions of unbelieving men. We know well enough that nuclear energy is theoretically capable of wiping out every form of life on this planet, including mankind. But we also know that such a catastrophe will never occur. We further know that the earth will never be inhabited by a degenerate race of off-human mutants made so by huge overdoses of radiation.

First, the Holy Scriptures tell us what we could never learn any other way: they tell us what we are, who we are, how we got here, why we are here and what we are required to do while we remain here. They trace our history from the begin-

THE TEACHINGS OF CHRIST   113

ning down to the present time and on into the
centuries and millenniums ahead. They track us
into the atomic age, through the space age and on
into the golden age. They reveal that at an appropriate time the direction of the world will be taken
away from men and placed in the hands of the
Man who alone has the wisdom and power to
rule it.

I omit here purposely the details. These are
given in satisfying fullness in the writings of the
holy prophets and apostles and in the words of
Christ spoken while He was yet among us. The
one great truth I would emphasize here is that after the warlords have shot their last missile and
dropped their last bomb there will still be living
men inhabiting this globe. After the world has
gone through the meat grinder of Armageddon,
the earth will still be inhabited by men; not by bio-
logical freaks, but by real people like you and me.

If the world can escape annihilation only by
adopting the ethics of Jesus we may as well resign
ourselves to the inevitable explosion, for a huge
block of the earth's population is controlled by
Communists whose basic ideology is violently
anti-Christian and who are determined to extir-
pate every trace of Christianity from among
them. Other large blocks are non-Christian and
grimly set to remain so. The West, it is true, pays
lip service to Christianity, but selfishness, greed,
ambition, pride and lust rule the rulers of these
lands almost to a man. While they will now and
then speak well of Christ, yet the total quality of

their conduct leaves little doubt that they are not much influenced by His teachings.

The hope that the nations will accept the ethics of Jesus, disarm and live like brothers is utterly unrealistic and naive. In the first place the teachings of Jesus were never intended for the nations of the world. Our Lord sent His followers into all the world to make and baptize disciples. These disciples were to be taught to observe the commandments of Christ. They would thus become a minority group, a peculiar people, in the world but not of it, sometimes tolerated but more often despised and persecuted. And history demonstrates that this is exactly what happened wherever groups of people took the gospel seriously.

To expect of once-born nations conduct possible only to the regenerated, purified, Spirit-led followers of Christ is to confuse the truth of Christianity and hope for the impossible. In the Scriptures the nations of the earth are symbolized by the lion, the bear and the leopard. Christians, in sharp contrast, are likened to peaceful sheep in the midst of wolves, who manage to stay alive only by keeping close to the Shepherd. If the sheep will not act like the bear, why should we expect the bear to act like the sheep?

It might be well for us Christians to listen less to the news commentators and more to the voice of the Spirit. And the inspired prophets will prove a fine antidote to the uninspired scientists.

The Decline of Good Reading

The reading habits of the average evangelical Christian in the United States, as far as I have been able to observe them, are so wretchedly bad as actually to arrest the spiritual development of the individual believer and block the progress of the faith he professes to hold.

So powerful is the effect of the printed page on human character that the reading of good books is not only a privilege but an obligation, and the habitual reading of poor ones a positive tragedy.

Of course I do not here refer to the output of the yellow press. I think we may safely assume that no true Christian would stoop to read the under-the-counter literary obscenities of the corner newsstand or the hole-in-the-wall bookstore. By "poor" books I mean the religious trash being turned out these days by the various publishers under the name of Christian. Tons of this stuff are produced each year to satisfy a market which a previous output has in large measure helped to create.

This religious rubbish is mostly fiction and serves three ends: It helps to fatten the bank account of the evangelical "novelist" who writes it; it keeps the publishers in business, and it feeds the depraved, or at least underdeveloped, appetites of the demi-Christians who find serious reading hard going but who lap up the denatured pabulum of the press as avidly as a kitten laps cream. And if I were allowed a choice I would go along with the kitten, for cream is both tasty and nutritious, while the average religious novel is wholly lacking in nutriment and is found palatable only by those persons whose taste buds have been debauched by prolonged exposure to Christian literature which is, if the truth were told, neither Christian nor literature.

Were a Christian to backslide and read a bad book secretly, as the proverbial schoolboy is said to read the dime novel behind his geography book, one could hope that he might later come to himself and leave the swine pen for the father's house; but what are we to say when bad books become part of the approved curriculum for evangelical Christians in almost all churches? What can we do when books of a mental level not above nine years are hailed as masterworks and given rave reviews in the religious press? What are we to say when the melodramatic love stories and spine-chilling adventures of a generation ago are retold by our modern religious writers with a bit of pious dialogue sandwiched in between torrid love embraces or "drop-thet-gun podner" artificialities to sanctify what would otherwise be a wholly evil production?

Being free from external compulsion, the Christian public quite naturally reads what it likes; and apparently it likes inferior religious literature. Should the conscience protest against the waste of time and energy involved in chronic addiction to literary trivialities, it is soon subverted by the argument that practically everyone approves such stuff, almost all religious publishers produce it and all the bookstores sell it. So what chance does one feeble conscience have against such tremendous odds?

All this accords with the false philosophy current among us which holds that to read anything religious is better than nothing, so we continue to produce literary mediocrities, vapid, amateurish, illiterate, and dedicated to the proposition that anything goes if only somewhere in the book someone makes the point that everybody ought to be born again. No matter how impossible the book in style and substance, if it puts in a dutiful plug for the gospel now and then, the evangelical leaders will bless it with their imprimatur and *nihil obstat*. Indeed it is hardly too much to say that illiterate religious literature has now become the earmark of evangelicalism. It is lamentable that we are content to leave quality to the Catholic and the liberal.

Why does the gospel Christian of today find the reading of great books almost beyond him? Is the intellectual capacity of the evangelical of today inferior to that of his spiritual progenitor of two hundred years ago?

The answer to the first question is somewhat complicated, but the second can be answered easily and correctly with an emphatic No. Intellectual powers do not wane from one generation to another. We are as smart as our forefathers. Any thought they could entertain we can entertain if we are sufficiently interested to make the effort.

The major cause of the decline in the quality of current Christian literature is not intellectual; it is spiritual. To enjoy a great religious work requires a degree of consecration to God and detachment from the world that few modern Christians have experienced. The early Christian Fathers, the mystics, the Puritans, are not hard to understand, but they inhabit the highlands where the air is crisp and rarefied and none but the God-enamored can come.

Rather than climb the mountain we choose to dig our shallow caves a few feet above the floor of the valley. Our spiritual moods and emotions are degraded. We eat and drink and rise up to play. We take our religious instruction in the form of stories, and anything that requires meditation bores us. And writers and publishers contribute to our delinquency by providing us with plenty of religious nothing to satisfy our carnal appetite.

O ye Americans, our mouth is open unto you, our heart is enlarged!

"Give attendance to reading . . ." (1 Timothy 4:13).

The Way of the Cross

"Things have come to a pretty pass," said a famous Englishman testily, "when religion is permitted to interfere with our private lives."

To which we may reply that things have come to a worse pass when an intelligent man living in a Protestant country could make such a remark. Had this man never read the New Testament? Had he never heard of Stephen? or Paul? or Peter? Had he never thought about the millions who followed Christ cheerfully to violent death, sudden or lingering, because they did allow their religion to interfere with their private lives?

But we must leave this man to his conscience and his Judge and look into our own hearts. Maybe he but expressed openly what some of us feel secretly. Just how radically has our religion interfered with the neat pattern of our own lives? Perhaps we had better answer that question first.

I have long believed that a man who spurns the Christian faith outright is more respected before God and the heavenly powers than the man who pretends to religion but refuses to come under its total domination. The first is an overt enemy, the second a false friend. It is the latter who will be spewed out of the mouth of Christ; and the reason is not hard to understand.

One picture of a Christian is a man carrying a cross. "If any man will come after me, let him deny himself, and take up his cross daily, and follow me" (Luke 9:23). The man with a cross no longer controls his destiny; he lost control when he picked up his cross. That cross immediately became to him an all-absorbing interest, an overwhelming interference. No matter what he may desire to do, there is but one thing he can do; that is, move on toward the place of crucifixion.

The man who will not brook interference is under no compulsion to follow Christ. "If any man will," said our Lord, and thus freed every man and placed the Christian life in the realm of voluntary choice.

Yet no man can escape interference. Law, duty, hunger, accident, natural disasters, illness, death, all intrude into his plans, and in the long run there is nothing he can do about it. Long experience with the rude necessities of life has taught men that these interferences will be thrust upon them sooner or later, so they learn to make what terms they can with the inevitable. They learn how to stay within the narrow circular rabbit path where the least interference is to be found. The bolder ones may challenge the world, enlarge the circle somewhat and so increase the number of their problems, but no one invites trouble deliberately. Human nature is not built that way.

Truth is a glorious but hard mistress. She never consults, bargains or compromises. She cries from the top of the high places, "Receive my instruction, and not silver; and knowledge rather than choice gold." After that, every man is on his own. He may accept or refuse, receive or set at naught as he pleases; and there will be no attempt at coercion, though the man's whole destiny is at stake.

Let a man become enamored of Eternal Wisdom and set his heart to win her, and he takes on himself a full-time, all engaging pursuit. Thereafter he will have room for little else. Thereafter his whole life will be filled with seekings and findings, self-repudiations, tough disciplines and daily dyings as he is being crucified unto the world and the world unto him.

Were this an unfallen world the path of truth would be a smooth and easy one. Had the nature of man not suffered a huge moral dislocation there would be no discord between the way of God and the way of man. I assume that in heaven the angels live through a thousand serene millenniums without feeling the slightest discord between their desires and the will of God. But not so among men on earth. Here the natural man receives not the things of the Spirit of God; the flesh lusts against the Spirit, and the Spirit against the flesh, and these are contrary one to the other. In that contest there can be only one outcome. We must surrender and God must have His way. His glory and our eternal welfare require that it be so.

Another reason that our religion must interfere with our private lives is that we live in the world, the Bible name for human society. The regenerated man has been inwardly separated from society as Israel was separated from Egypt at the crossing of the Red Sea. The Christian is a man of heaven temporarily living on earth. Though in spirit divided from the race of fallen men he must yet in the flesh live among them. In many things he is like them, but in others he differs so radically from them that they cannot but see and resent it. From the days of Cain and Abel the man of earth has punished the man of heaven for being different. The long history of persecution and martyrdom confirms this.

But we must not get the impression that the Christian life is one continuous conflict, one unbroken irritating struggle against the world, the flesh and the devil. A thousand times no. A heart that learns to die with Christ soon knows the blessed experience of rising with Him, and all the world's persecutions cannot still the high note of holy joy that springs up in the soul that has become the dwelling place of the Holy Spirit.

CHAPTER

30

Needed: A Reformation within the Church

The first look of the church is toward Christ, who is her Head, her Lord and her All.

After that she must be self-regarding and world-regarding, with a proper balance between the two.

By self-regarding I do not mean self-centered. I mean that the church must examine herself constantly to see if she be in the faith; she must engage in severe self-criticism with a cheerful readiness to make amends; she must live in a state of perpetual penitence, seeking God with her whole heart; she must constantly check her life and conduct against the Holy Scriptures and bring her life into line with the will of God.

By world-regarding I mean that the church must know why she is here on earth; that she

123

must acknowledge her indebtedness to all mankind (Romans 1:14–15); that she must take seriously the words of her Lord, "Go ye into all the world and preach the gospel to every creature," and "Ye shall be witnesses unto me both in Jerusalem, and in all Judea, and in Samaria, and unto the uttermost part of the earth."

The task of the church is twofold: to spread Christianity throughout the world and to make sure that the Christianity she spreads is the pure New Testament kind.

Theoretically the seed, being the Word of God, should produce the same kind of fruit regardless of the spiritual condition of those who scatter it; but it does not work that way. The identical message preached to the heathen by men of differing degrees of godliness will produce different kinds of converts and result in a quality of Christianity varying according to the purity and power of those who preach it.

Christianity will always reproduce itself after its kind. A worldly-minded, unspiritual church, when she crosses the ocean to give her witness to peoples of other tongues and other cultures, is sure to bring forth on other shores a Christianity much like her own.

Not the naked Word only but the character of the witness determines the quality of the convert. The church can do no more than transplant herself. What she is in one land she will be in another. A crab apple does not become a Grimes Golden by being carried from one country to another.

God has written His law deep into all life; everything must bring forth after its kind.

The popular notion that the first obligation of the church is to spread the gospel to the uttermost parts of the earth is false. Her first obligation is to be spiritually worthy to spread it. Our Lord said "Go," but He also said "Wait," and the waiting had to come before the going. Had the disciples gone forth as missionaries before the day of Pentecost, it would have been an overwhelming spiritual disaster, for they could have done no more than make converts after their own likeness, and this would have altered for the worse the whole history of the Western world and had consequences throughout the ages to come.

To spread an effete, degenerate brand of Christianity to pagan lands is not to fulfill the commandment of Christ or to discharge our obligation to the heathen. These terrible words of Jesus haunt my soul: "For ye compass sea and land to make one proselyte, and when he is made, ye make him twofold more the child of hell than yourselves" (Matthew 23:15).

To win men of Judaism from among the Gentile nations was altogether a good and right thing to do. Thousands of happy converts were won to the religion of Moses during the years of Israel's spiritual ascendancy; but at the time of Christ Judaism had sunk so low that her missionary effort wrought actual harm instead of good.

It would appear logical that a subnormal, powerless church would not engage in missionary activity, but again the facts contradict the theory. Christian groups that have long ago lost every trace of moral fire nevertheless continue to grow at home and reproduce themselves in other lands. Indeed there is scarcely a fringe sect or heretical cult these days but is enjoying amazing success among the backward peoples of the world.

The evangelical wing of the church has in recent years become world-regarding to a remarkable degree. Within the last twenty years evangelical missionary activity on foreign fields has been stepped up tremendously. But there is in the whole thing one dangerous weakness. That weakness is the naive assumption that we have only to reach the last tribe with our brand of Christianity and the world has been evangelized. This is an assumption that we dare not make.

Evangelical Christianity, at least in the United States, is now tragically below the New Testament standard. Worldliness is an accepted part of our way of life. Our religious mood is social instead of spiritual. We have lost the art of worship. We are not producing saints. Our models are successful businessmen, celebrated athletes and theatrical personalities. We carry on our religious activities after the methods of the modern advertiser. Our homes have been turned into theaters. Our literature is shallow and our hymnody borders on sacrilege. And scarcely anyone appears to care. We must have a better kind of Christian soon or within another half century we may have no true Christianity at all. Increased numbers of demi-Christians is not enough. We must have a reformation.

CHAPTER

31

The Perils of Too Much Liberty

F reedom is priceless and where it is present
    almost any kind of life is enjoyable. When it
is absent life can never be enjoyed; it can only be
endured.

Though millions have died in freedom's defense
and though her praise is in everyone's mouth, yet
she has been tragically misunderstood by her advocates and sorely wounded in the house of her
friends. I think the difficulty lies with our failure to
distinguish freedom from liberty, which are indeed
sisters but not identical twins.

Freedom is liberty within bounds: liberty to
obey holy laws, liberty to keep the commandments of Christ, to serve mankind, to develop to
the full all the latent possibilities within our redeemed natures. True Christian liberty never sets

us free to indulge our lusts or to follow our fallen impulses.

The desire for unqualified freedom caused the fall of Lucifer and wrought the destruction of the angels that sinned. These sought freedom to do as they willed, and to get it they threw away the beautiful liberty that meant freedom to do the will of God. And the human race followed them in their tragic moral blunder.

To anyone who bothers to think a bit it should be evident that there is in the universe no such thing as absolute freedom. Only God is free. It is inherent in creaturehood that its freedom must be limited by the will of the Creator and the nature of the thing created. The glory of heaven lies in the character of the freedom enjoyed by those who dwell therein. That innumerable company of angels, the general assembly and church of the First-born and the spirits of just men made perfect are at liberty to fulfill all the broad purposes of God, and this liberty secures for them an infinitely greater degree of happiness than unqualified freedom could do.

Unqualified freedom in any area of human life is deadly. In government it is anarchy, in domestic life free love, and in religion antinomianism. The freest cells in the body are cancer cells, but they kill the organism where they grow. A healthy society requires that its members accept a limited freedom. Each must curtail his own liberty that all may be free, and this law runs throughout all the created universe, including the kingdom of God.

Too much liberty weakens whatever it touches. The corn of wheat can bring forth fruit only as it waives its freedom and surrenders itself to the laws of nature. The robin may fly about all summer enjoying her freedom, but if she wants a nest full of fledglings she must sit for weeks a voluntary captive while the mystery of life gestates beneath her soft feathers. She has her choice: be free and barren or curtail her freedom and bring forth young.

Every man in a free society must decide whether he will exploit his liberty or curtail it for intelligent and moral ends. He may take upon him the responsibility of a business and a family and thus be useful to the race, or he may shun all obligations and end on skid row. The tramp is freer than president or king, but his freedom is his undoing. While he lives he remains socially sterile and when he dies he leaves behind him nothing to make the world glad he lived.

The Christian cannot escape the peril of too much liberty. He is indeed free, but his very freedom may prove a source of real temptation to him. He is free from the chains of sin, free from the moral consequences of evil acts now forgiven, free from the curse of the law and the displeasure of God. Grace has opened the prison door for him, and like Barabbas of old he walks at liberty because Another died in his stead.

All this the instructed Christian knows and he refuses to let false teachers and misguided religionists rivet a yoke of bondage upon his neck.

But now what shall he do with his freedom? Two possibilities offer themselves. He may accept his blood-won freedom as a cloak for the flesh, as the New Testament declares that some have done, or he may kneel like the camel to receive his voluntary burden. And what is this burden? The woes of his fellowmen which he must do what he can to assuage; the debt which he along with Paul owes to the lost world; the sound of hungry children crying in the night; the church in Babylonian captivity; the swift onrush of evil doctrines and the success of false prophets; the slow decay of the moral foundations of the so-called Christian nations and whatever else demands self-sacrifice, cross-carrying, long prayer vigils and courageous witness to alleviate and correct.

Christianity is the religion of freedom and democracy is freedom in organized society, but if we continue to misunderstand this freedom we may soon have neither Christianity or democracy. To protect political liberty free men must lay a voluntary obligation upon themselves; to preserve the religion of salvation by free grace a great many Christians must waive their right to be free and take upon themselves a load greater than they have ever carried before.

When in danger the state can conscript men to fight for her freedom, but there are no conscripts in the army of the Lord. To bear a cross the Christian must take it up of his own free will. No authority can compel us to feed the hungry or evangelize the lost or pray for revival or sacrifice ourselves for Christ's sake and the sake of suffering humanity.

The ideal Christian is one who knows he is free to do as he will and wills to be a servant. This is the path Christ took; blessed is the man who follows Him.

The Days of Our Years

A few days after these words appear in print the old year of our Lord will have gone to join the long procession of years and centuries that move on into the shadows of a past that can come no more.

In the year just gone the world has been writing history, not with ink only but with blood and tears; not in the quiet of the study but in violence, terror and death in city streets and along the borders of nations; and other and milder but more significant history has been written by incredible feats of power in sending man-made objects out to circle the moon and the sun.

But what is more important is that each of us has also been writing history. That the church has made history is not so significant as that you have and I have. What is done by a group is possible only because individuals have been at work. A company cannot work as a company nor will it be judged as such. Paul by inspiration singled out the individual and stood him up alone to receive judgment:

> Every man's work shall be made manifest; for the day shall declare it, because it shall be revealed by fire: and the fire shall try every man's work of what sort it is. If any man's work abide which he hath built thereupon, he shall receive a reward. If any man's work shall be burned, he shall suffer loss: but he himself shall be saved; yet so as by fire. (1 Corinthians 3:13-15)

And again,

> For we must all appear before the judgment seat of Christ; that every one may receive the things done in his body, according to that he hath done, whether it be good or bad. (2 Corinthians 5:10)

At that day there will be no hiding in the crowd. Each one will come carrying his own book of history under his arm. So we should close reverently the book of the year just gone; we shall see it again.

To each one fortunate enough to live out 1959, God will have given 365 days broken into 8,760 hours. Of these hours, 2,920 will have been spent in sleep, and about the same number at work. An equal number has been given us to spend in reverent preparation for the moment when days and years shall cease and time shall be no more. What prayer could be more spiritually appropriate than that of Moses, the man of God: "So teach us to number our days, that we may apply our hearts unto wisdom" (Psalm 90:12).

It is important that we remember that all our days come to us out of the sheer mercy of God, unearned, undeserved and, I fear, mostly unappreciated. By sin our lives stand under forfeit; God owes us nothing. The bell that tolls the death of the passing year might as justly toll for us. Only by God's infinite goodness are we yet alive to see each other's face. Each year is a gift of grace and each day an unearned bonus.

I think it is typical of us that we take our days for granted. We say at the start of each year, "This may be the last," and resolve to amend our lives; but before many days have passed we forget our resolutions and grow bold and arrogant again, deceived by the apparent prodigality with which our days are given to us, heaped up, shaken together and running over. But all things have an end. The pitcher goes once too often to the well; the old tree braves one too many storms and comes down with a great crash upon the hill; the strongest heart weakens at last and sputters to a stop.

It may have been at the shut of the year that Moses made his plaintive prayer for wisdom to know what to do with his days; and it was in his old age that Jacob stood before Pharaoh and confessed, "The days of the years of my pilgrimage are an hundred and thirty years: few and evil have the days of the years of my life been, and have not attained unto the days of the years of the life of my fathers in the days of their pilgrimage" (Genesis 47:9). These were wise men, disciplined, seasoned, familiar with the ways of men and experienced in the ways of God. They valued the days and the years. It is well that we learn to do the same.

Yet I do not advise that we end the year on a somber note. The march, not the dirge, has ever been the music of Christianity. If we are good students in the school of life, there is much that the years have to teach us. But the Christian is more than a student, more than a philosopher. He is a believer, and the object of his faith makes the difference, the mighty difference.

Of all persons the Christian should be best prepared for whatever the New Year brings. He has dealt with life at its source. In Christ he has disposed of a thousand enemies that other men must face alone and unprepared. He can face his tomorrow cheerful and unafraid because yesterday he turned his feet into the ways of peace and today he lives in God. The man who has made God his dwelling place will always have a safe habitation.

Charles Wesley, God's enraptured troubadour, wrote and sang a hymn for almost every occasion. On the morning of his birthday he composed a song of praise to God. Let us borrow it and adapt two of its stanzas to the birth of the New Year.

All honor and praise
To the Father of grace,
To the Spirit and Son I return;
The business pursue
He hath made me to do,
And rejoice that I ever was born.

My remnant of days
I spend in His praise,
Who died the whole world to redeem:
Be they many or few,
my days are His due,
And they all are devoted to Him.

CHAPTER

33

On Going through School
without Learning Anything

When we become Christians we enter the
school of Christ. We come under the direct
tutelage of the Holy Spirit and should move nor-
mally upward by stages toward spiritual perfection.
But the truth is most of us do not.

When the children of Israel came out of Egypt
they became students in God's school of experience, but they were slow to learn and sometimes
they did not learn at all or forgot at critical moments all that they had learned. The Old Testament is helpful reading, not because of any
worthy qualities it reveals about Israel but because in it we see the great kindness and
long-suffering of God toward a dull and wrong-
headed people who managed to go through
school without learning anything.

Because Israel could not or would not learn from experience they were at various times defeated, oppressed, dispossessed, and at last they were rejected outright and dispersed throughout the world. The presence of Jews in every corner of the world is a witness to this.

That Israel should have learned and did not is no proof that they were more obtuse than the rest of us; it proves rather that they were very much like us. Instead of smugly condemning a nation for its folly we had better consider ourselves lest we also fall. For the record of the church is no better than that of Israel. Before the last book of the New Testament had been finished the church had started through the same cycle of learning and forgetting, rising and falling, sinning and repenting that had marked Israel in earlier times. And after the passing of nineteen hundred years we are still at it.

A proverb has it that all we learn from history is that we learn nothing from history. The truth of this is demonstrated plainly in the records of religious denominations. Almost every denomination began as a revolt against theological error or formality in worship, worldliness in conduct, externalism or ecclesiastical tyranny. A discontented man of great spiritual desire was joined by a few others of like mind. These had or soon received clear religious experience that gave urgency to their witness and zeal to their efforts. Usually they threw off the burden of religious complexities and turned to simplicity and inwardness. So great was the relief that those who

rushed to join them felt that they had indeed re-
captured the glory of the Early Church, and not
one of them would have believed that their precious God-enamored band of Christians could
ever forget.

But they did. Or if they did not, the next generation did. It is one of the anomalies of religion that
the second generation members of a spiritual
movement usually go back to the bondage from
which their fathers escaped such a short while before. With many sad examples to warn them they
yet move as if hypnotized or sleepwalking
straight back into captivity. They will not learn
from others' experience.

The same is true of local churches. Many of the
very persons who flee the worldly confusion of a
dead church for the spiritual freedom of a live one
will, when elected to places of influences in the
new fellowship, soon begin to introduce into that
fellowship the identical practices that killed their
former church and drove them from it. Little by
little every unscriptural abuse, every idol, every
golden calf will appear to grieve the Spirit and stifle the life of the people. And nothing anyone can
say will halt this march back into the twilight.

The school into which we Christians are introduced furnishes many lessons, all taught by the
wisest of all teachers; but everything depends
upon how we respond to them. Unfortunately
many of us learn little and soon forget what little
we may have learned. We can hear great preaching, as Demas heard Paul, without profit; we can

meet saintly Christians without becoming stimulated to seek to live holier lives; we can see miraculous answers to prayer and be none the better for it. The providential circumstances set up the lessons; the Teacher is wise and patient; only the disciple fails to profit.

A child who through negligence learns nothing in school is guilty of practicing serious waste. He is wasting the money furnished by his parents or the taxpayers, and the gifts and energies of everyone associated with the effort to teach him are wasted as well. And much the same thing may be said of the dullard Christian. He is wasting the painstaking efforts of every pastor or teacher who tries to help him.

There have been a few noble souls who have managed to break through into a place of great spiritual power and purity with scarcely anyone to help them and with but the scantiest educational equipment to assist them in their search for God and holy things. Ought we not to be ashamed who are surrounded with such a wealth of aids and still learn so little?

And how much suffering is wasted on us. Chastisement is a stern teacher, but there are great riches to be gained in her school. It is critically important that we enter that school with humble hearts and open minds.

Yes, it is possible to go through school without learning anything. For all of us the final bell will ring soon. We had better do some hard studying before that time comes.

The Deadliest Sins of All

Agreat preacher, now deceased, to whom I used often to listen with profit and delight, would sometimes shout dramatically, "God never classifies sin."

His words were intended as a protest against a careless attitude toward certain forms of sin, and in their context I agree with them. Nevertheless God does classify sin and so does the law of the land, and so does the conscience of every man.

As various serpents differ from each other in their power to kill, so various sins carry different kinds of venom, all bad, but not all equally bad, their power to injure depending upon the high or low concentration of iniquity they carry in them.

Within the precincts of religion are sometimes found certain sins which I want here to mention. These may be classified under three heads: Sins committed out of weakness, respectable sins more or less allowed by everyone, and sins that have been woven into the religious fabric until they have become a necessary part of it.

No sin is to be excused. Every sin carries its own penalty. But the sin committed on impulse or the sin committed out of weakness over the protests of the heart surely does not carry the same deadly charge as those done with brazen deliberation. From such a sin there is complete deliverance by the power of Christ; and from such there is more likely to be, since it is a grief to those who commit it.

Sins of the second category are those that exist with the sanction of or at least the connivance of the church, such as pride, vanity, self-centeredness, levity, worldliness, gluttony, the telling of "white" lies, borderline dishonesty, lack of compassion for the unfortunate, complacency, absorption in the affairs of this life, love of pleasure, the holding of grudges, stinginess, gossiping and various dirty habits not expressly forbidden by name in the Scriptures.

These sins are so common that they have been accepted as normal by the average church and are either not mentioned at all or referred to in smiling half-humor by the clergy. While not as spectacular as a roaring weekend drunk or as dramatic as a violent explosion of temper, they are in the long run more deadly than either, for they are seldom recognized as sin and are practically never repented of. They remain year after year to grieve the Spirit and sap the life of the church, while everyone continues to speak the words of the true faith and go through the motions of perfunctory godliness, not knowing that there is anything wrong.

There is another kind of sin which for sheer turpitude must rate before those mentioned and very near to the sin that is unpardonable. It is the kind that has become incorporated into the structure of popular religion and is necessary to its success. From this kind of sin I have never known anyone to turn away after it got working for him. It appears to destroy its victims utterly.

So no one will be left guessing let me be specific. I refer to the methods used by various leaders to promote Christianity, by means of which they gain some kind of success but which are themselves basically evil. Here are a few examples:

Telling falsehoods about the size of crowds, the number responding to the invitation and the impression made upon the city. Using the tricks of psychology known to every showman, piously pretending that they are the very workings of the Holy Spirit. Humbly praying for things in the presence of persons known to be well off and suggestible, and then devoutly testifying to answered prayer. Building a big reputation for being men of faith when the whole procedure is based upon a shrewd knowledge of human nature. Retaining publicity men to keep their names before the public and allowing the impression to get abroad that it is all the result of spontaneous public interest.

Still other deadly sins exist within the very circles that make pretense of the most advanced type of godliness; such, for instance, as professing great compassion for the sick, conducting giant meetings for the purpose of bringing healing to them, but slyly separating the hopeless cases from those less serious and more susceptible to psychological impressions, and all the while growing rich on the miseries and pains of humanity. Some of these prophets own large estates, drive huge cars and boast of fabulous wealth tied up in equipment, while the suffering multitudes whose blood they suck hobble or crawl or are carried to meetings.

Investigation of one such man carried on by some godly pastors revealed that he had been hiring healthy persons to come up for prayer and pretend to be healed. This was done, he explained when faced with the deed, to "encourage weak faith." Thus lying and deception were deliberately made a part of the purported methods of the Holy Spirit.

Others base everything on the power of money and personality, yet testify that they are trusting wholly in the power of the Spirit. And many introduce into their religious work every gimmick known to the world, and so destroy the very thing they profess to cherish.

It is sufficient evidence of the moral insensibility of such men that they violently resent even the mention of these things; and it is further proof of the success of their methods that the very public they have betrayed will rush to defend them.

Conformity, a Snare in Religion

C onformity is the virtue of the slave and can become the vice of the saint.

It is a gloomy lesson of history that whole populations will often enslave themselves to the will of an ambitious political leader if he can promise them security and a few pennies more wages per day. And as often as not, after they have sold their birthright to him by conformity they find that they get the few extra pennies only by long hours of toil, and that the security they need most is protection from their protector.

The dictator, whether he be a political or a religious one, must be able to distribute little favors to the faithful, and these he always manages to have at hand. These favors are like the fish tossed to the performing seal, or like the salt lick of early American days placed near the shooting blind to entice the wary deer within range of the old muzzleloader. But conformity is what the dictator must have if he is to do any dictating worth speaking of.

Now, conformity within limits is a good thing. The musician must conform to the laws of harmony, the engineer to the laws of physics and the farmer to the law of growing things. If I would learn a new language I must bow to its grammar, its vocabulary and its idiom. And civilized society is possible only because the majority of citizens conform quietly to the rules of civilized life.

When this has been said in praise of conformity, there is not much left to say about it that is good. From there on it is almost wholly evil. It is evil because it can be and often is used by the dominant few to enslave the pliable many.

Almost every great soul has been a nonconformist. Millions of us less gifted persons may thank God for the sturdy dissenters who fought our battles for us, often long before we were born, by daring to rise up and challenge the status quo.

Every gain made in the field of government was made not by the masses but by a few nonconformists who put their lives on the line and refused to accept the leadership of men unworthy to lead. The curators of the status quo rolled horrified eyes to heaven and appealed to the God they conceived to be the protector of the comfortable to save their unearned positions and their well-lined nests from these vulgar malcontents. But their prayers were not heard. God was on the side of the dissenters. The measure of freedom we of the Western world enjoy today is a gift to us from God—and from our nonconforming forebears.

We Protestants owe our religious freedom and the blessing of an open Bible to men whose sepulchers we now delight to build, but whom we might not so willingly have aided if we had lived at the time when the outcome of their struggles was in doubt.

Conformity to the Word of God is always right, but obedience to religious leaders is good only if those leaders prove themselves worthy to lead. Leadership in the church of Christ is a spiritual thing and should be so understood by everyone. It takes more than a ballot to make a leader.

There is great danger in our present-day evangelical circles that we place too great importance on conformity to authorities within the churches and so stifle whatever originality and daring there may be among us. That denomination is in grave peril when the only virtue required of its ministers is conformity and the only unforgivable ecclesiastical sin is insubordination.

This situation develops when church authorities are placed in office by machinery instead of being commissioned by the Holy Spirit. To stay in the ascendancy these leaders must demand and get conformity to protect rules on the part of those under them. Such as these would far rather preside over a denomination of mediocre conformists than to be embarrassed by the pres-

ence of anointed men of vision who might un-
wittingly steal the hearts of the people from
them. Thus when a head appears slightly above
the dead level of flat conformity it is gently
lopped off, ostensibly to protect the work of the
Lord, but actually to retain control of the ecclesiastical machine.

No Spirit-led man is afraid of losing his position
in a Spirit-filled church. Where the church is conceived to be no more than an institution, then every man honored by a place on the hierarchical
totem pole will seek to preserve his treasured
niche, or to secure a higher one. Then he will look
for a technique for survival, and over the years
imposed conformity has been the one most frequently employed by the largest number.

If the church is to prosper spiritually she must
have spiritual leadership, not leadership by majority vote. It is highly significant that when the
apostle Paul found it necessary to ask for obedience among the young churches he never appealed to them on the grounds that he had been
duly elected to office. He asserted his authority as
an apostle appointed by the Head of the church.
He held his position by right of sheer spiritual ascendancy, the only earthly right that should be
honored among the children of the new creation.

In the church or denomination where the Holy
Spirit is in control there will be no imposed conformity, but there will be happy cooperation with the
anointed leaders on the part of all. The rank-and-
file soldiers of the King will recognize their true

leaders; they will be the ones not with the epaulets on their shoulders but with the oil on their foreheads.

The Popularity of Christ

One of the most incredible phenomena in the world today is the immense and universal popularity of Jesus Christ.

Almost all of the major religions are friendly to Him, and even those who do not own His deity are respectful toward Him. Practically every cult finds a place for Him somewhere in its system. Philosophy, psychology, science—all quote Him with approval. Big business, which operates according to principles exactly opposite to everything He taught, continually genuflects before him. The entertainment world purrs over Him, and the image of Him it projects is always warm and attractive. His name carries a charm for politicians and prize fighters, as well as for Scout leaders and P.T.A. presidents. He is the one figure that consistently overshadows such historical heroes as Abraham Lincoln and such current celebrities as Dag Hammarskjold and Albert Schweitzer. His prestige remains consistently at the top, no matter who may for the moment be getting the headlines.

Yet the teachings of Christ are wholly contrary to the beliefs of the modern world. The spiritual philosophy underlying the kingdom of God is radically opposed to that of civilized society. In short, the Christ of the New Testament and the world of mankind are so sharply opposed to each other as to amount to downright hostility. To achieve a compromise is impossible.

We can only conclude that Jesus is universally popular today because He is universally misunderstood.

Everyone admires Jesus, but almost no one takes Him seriously. He is considered a kindly idealist who loved babies and underprivileged persons. He is pictured as a gentle dreamer who was naive enough to believe in human goodness and brave enough to die for His belief. The world thinks of Him as meek, selfless and loving, and values Him because He was what we all are at heart, or would be if things were not so tough and we had more time to cultivate our virtues. Or He is a sweet, holy symbol of something too fine, too beautiful, to be real, but something which we would not lose nevertheless from our treasure house of precious things.

Because the human mind has two compartments, the practical and the ideal, people are able to live comfortably with their dreamy, romantic conception of Jesus while paying no attention whatsoever to His words. It is this neat division between the fanciful and the real that enables countless thousands of persons to say "Lord, Lord" in all sincerity while living every moment in flat defiance of His authority.

Were someone to rise in the General Assembly of the United Nations and pay a tribute to Jesus Christ probably no one present, not even a Communist, would object. But let a delegate suggest that a disputed point be settled by appeal to the teachings of Christ and he would be voted down with derision. Christ is all right as a moral ornament, but no one in that august body is willing that he should be anything more.

This is not to be wondered at. The United Nations is Adam organized. It is a last-day effort to build a tower of security that will reach unto heaven. The first man Adam is trying to establish something on the flesh that will endure through the centuries, and the last Adam declares it cannot be done. The last Adam, Christ, is popular with the first Adam only because His teachings are almost wholly unknown to the men of this world and He Himself is completely misunderstood.

In the working out of God's eternal purpose the society of the first Adam and the society of the last Adam, though utterly opposed, may for a while coexist, but not for long (Hebrews 12:26–27). The flesh may admire the spirit while refusing to go along with it, or it may misunderstand the spirit and believe that it is itself spiritual while actually sunk in corruption.

The latter, I believe, explains the present popularity of Christ in the world. The contradiction between Christ and unregenerate society is sharp and irreconcilable, but the contrast between society and its own mistaken conception of Him is scarcely noticeable. So the world can cherish its image of Christ and ignore His commandments without a qualm of conscience.

What should seriously concern us, however, is not that the world praises Christ without obeying Him, but that the church does. The men of this world go their way careless of the teachings of Christ, but in doing so they are consistent with their position. They have made no vows to the Lord nor taken His name upon them. But when a Christian ignores the commandment of Christ, he is guilty of sin doubly compounded. He violates holy vows, is guilty of rebellion against God and commits the grotesque sin of calling Jesus Lord with his words and denying His Lordship with his deeds.

Should anyone doubt that Christians, even Bible Christians, habitually ignore the teachings of Christ, let him rise in a business meeting of his church or denomination and quote a passage from the sayings of our Lord as the final authority on a question before the house. He will soon learn how little the words of Christ influence the thinking of the average delegate.

Christians today have developed the perilous habit of accepting the authority of the New Testament on matters that do not concern them and rejecting it on matters that do. And so with too many churches also Jesus is popular but impotent. Surely another reformation is indicated.

The Lordship of the Man Jesus Is Basic

We are under constant temptation these days to substitute another Christ for the Christ of the New Testament. The whole drift of modern religion is toward such a substitution.

To avoid this we must hold steadfastly to the concept of Christ as set forth so clearly and plainly in the Scriptures of truth. Though an angel from heaven should preach anything less than the Christ of the apostles let him be forthrightly and fearlessly rejected.

The mighty, revolutionary message of the Early Church was that a man named Jesus who had been crucified was now raised from the dead and exalted to the right hand of God. "Therefore, let all the house of Israel know assuredly, that God

hath made that same Jesus, whom ye have crucified, both Lord and Christ" (Acts 2:36).

Less than three hundred years after Pentecost
the hard-pressed defenders of the faith drew up a
manifesto condensing those teachings of the New
Testament having to do with the nature of Christ.
This manifesto declares that Christ is

> God of the substance of His Father, begot-
> ten before all ages: Man of the substance of
> His mother, born in the world: perfect God
> and perfect Man, of a reasonable soul and
> human flesh subsisting: Equal to His Fa-
> ther, as touching His Godhead: less than
> the Father, as touching His manhood.
> Who, although He be God and man, yet
> He is not two, but one Christ. One, not by
> conversion of the Godhead into flesh, but
> by the taking of the manhood into God.
> One altogether, not by the confusion of
> substance, but by the unity of Person. For
> as the reasonable soul and flesh is one
> man, so God and man is one Christ.

Even among those who acknowledge the deity
of Christ there is often a failure to recognize His
manhood. We are quick to assert that when He
walked the earth He was *God with men*, but we
overlook a truth equally as important, that where
He sits now on His mediatorial throne He is *Man
with God*.

The teaching of the New Testament is that now, at this very moment, there is a Man in heaven appearing in the presence of God for us. He is as certainly a man as was Adam or Moses or Paul. He is a man glorified, but His glorification did not dehumanize Him. Today He is a real man, of the race of mankind, bearing our lineaments and dimensions, a visible and audible man whom any other man would recognize instantly as one of us.

But more than this, He is heir of all things, Lord of all worlds, Head of the Church and the First-born of the new creation. He is the way to God, the life of the believer, the hope of Israel and the high priest of every true worshiper. He holds the keys of death and hell and stands as advocate and surety for everyone who believes on Him in truth.

This is not all that can be said about Him, for were all said that might be said I suppose the world itself could not contain the books that should be written. But this in brief is the Christ we preach to sinners as their only escape from the wrath to come. With Him rest the noblest hopes and dreams of men. All the longings for immortality that rise and swell in the human breast will be fulfilled in Him or they will never know fulfillment. There is no other way (John 14:6).

Salvation comes not by "accepting the finished work" or "deciding for Christ." It comes by believing on the Lord Jesus Christ, the whole, living, victorious Lord who, as God and man, fought our fight and won it, accepted our debt as His own and paid it, took our sins and died under them and rose again to set us free. This is the true Christ, and nothing less will do.

But something less is among us, nevertheless, and we do well to identify it so that we may repudiate it. That something is a poetic fiction, a product of the romantic imagination and maudlin religious fancy. It is a Jesus, gentle, dreamy, shy, sweet and feminine, almost effeminate, and marvelously adaptable to whatever society He may find Himself in. He is cooed over by women disappointed in love, patronized by pro tem celebrities and recommended by psychiatrists as a model of a well-integrated personality. He is used as a means to almost any carnal end, but he is never acknowledged as Lord. These quasi Christians follow a quasi Christ. They want his help but not his interference. They will flatter him but never obey him.

The argument of the apostles is that the man Jesus has been made higher than angels, higher than Moses and Aaron, higher than any creature in earth or heaven. And this exalted position He attained *as a man*. As God He already stood infinitely above all other beings. No argument was needed to prove the transcendence of the Godhead. The apostles were not declaring the preeminence of God, which would have been superfluous, but of a man, which was necessary.

Those first Christians believed that Jesus of Nazareth, a man they knew, had been raised to a position of Lordship over the universe. He was still their friend, still one of them, but had left them for a while to appear in the presence of God on their behalf. And the proof of this was the presence of the Holy Spirit among them.

One cause of our moral weakness today is an inadequate Christology. We think of Christ as God but fail to conceive of Him as a man glorified. To recapture the power of the Early Church we must believe what they believed. And they believed they had a God-approved man representing them in heaven.

38

The Menace of the Common Image

These middle years of the twentieth century will undoubtedly be known in history as the period of widespread democracy, phony and otherwise but always strongly influenced by socialism.

A lot of leveling has been going on among us lately, but, as Dr. Samuel Johnson noted in his day, the levelers always want to level down to themselves, never up. And since most of our self-anointed levelers begin pretty well down to scale, the total effect on society has not been to elevate, but to degrade.

Everyone acquainted with the English language knows that the word common may also mean vulgar and often does. The vulgar person is one of low tastes who is not only coarse and boorish but enjoys being so, and because his kind is often in the majority he is also said to be common. And it is this common fellow who has, unfortunately, become the model for the masses in human society.

The present clamor after a college education by such large numbers of our young people suggests that perhaps people are getting tired of being common and aspire to loftier and nobler lives. But this is an illusion. Whatever advanced education may do for us theoretically, it is a fact that the stream of college graduates being poured each year into the social current is not having the slightest ennobling effect upon society. It is rather the other way around; society quickly brings the graduate around to its way of thinking and living.

Vulgarity is a disease of the human spirit and is not cured by education, or travel, or familiarity with grand opera or works of art. Vulgarity may speak good English and live in a split-level house, but it is known for what it is by its attitudes, its morals, and its aspirations, or lack of them.

The true Christian is uncommon for the reason that he is not in the majority; he is as different from the world in which he lives as Abraham was different from the inhabitants of Canaan. He is likely to be a lowly, humble, approachable man with no claims to greatness or superiority, but his moral standards, his attitudes toward fame, money, earthly pleasures, life and death, mark him as a being from another world.

It is custom that destroys aspiration and turns every man into a copy of every other. "Woe unto thee, thou stream of human custom," wrote Augustine. "Who shall stay thy course? How long shall it be before thou art dried up? How long wilt thou carry down the sons of Eve into that huge and formidable ocean, which even they who are embarked on the cross can scarce pass over? . . . And yet, thou stream of hell, into thee are cast the sons of men."

The mighty error of the world has been to take for granted what someone has called "the rightness of the customary." The values, attitudes and practices of the majority in any given period constitute a code accepted as binding upon all members of society. Any aberration from this code on the part of anyone excites immediate attention and may even bring the charge of being "mentally ill." And unless I miss my guess I believe that the advocates of the customary are preparing to use the threat of being charged with mental illness as a whip to bring everyone into line. Incidentally, they tried that on Jesus and it did not work.

It is a law of the human soul that people tend to become like that which they admire most intensely. Deep and long continued admiration can alter the whole texture of the mind and heart and turn the devotee into something quite other than he was before.

For this reason it is critically important that we Christians should have right models. It is not enough to say that our model should be Christ. While that is true, it is also true that Christ is known mostly through the lives of His professed followers, and the more prominent and vocal these followers are the more powerful will be their influence upon the rank and file of Christians. If the models are imperfect the whole standard of Christian living must suffer as a result.

A sacred obligation lies upon each of us to be Christlike. This generation of Christians must have models it can safely admire. That is not the primary reason for seeking to be holy, but it is a powerful one. Many beginners are taking us for their examples. Later they will become detached from us and will learn to fix their eyes directly upon the Lord Himself; in the meantime, for better or for worse we are their idea of what Christ is like. This is a wonderful and frightening fact that we must face and deal with as we may.

We are under deep obligation to do all in our power to shatter the "common" image which is now accepted as standard for men in and out of the church. The nations need uncommon men to guide them and the church needs uncommon Christians. And we had better take this whole thing seriously.

Satan's Defeat Linked to His Moral Folly

T he devil is wise, and shrewdness is all that we may properly attribute to him, since sound moral judgment is an ingredient of wisdom and this the devil does not possess.

Further thought might require that we modify our belief that he is shrewd in any other than the most superficial meaning of the word: for shrewdness carries with it ability to plan ahead successfully, and apparently the devil is unable to do this. The truly shrewd man does not get caught in his own trap, but the devil has been caught in his not once but many times.

A shrewd strategist knows when to attack and when to call off the attack and withdraw. This the devil never seems to know. Bible history will show that he frequently went too far and defeated his own purposes over and over again.

One example of this was the heat he turned on the Hebrews in Egypt. Pharaoh had a pretty neat thing going (from his standpoint) when he managed to get all the able-bodied men among the Hebrews to work for him free. A great army of laborers was busy making bricks for the vast building activities of Egypt, and these bricks were costing Pharaoh not one cent. They were being made by slave labor. Had Pharaoh been wise, or even shrewd, he would have eased the pressure on the Hebrews a little and so continued to enjoy the benefits of their free labor for years to come. Instead he imposed impossible terms, drove the afflicted Hebrews to their knees and brought God to their rescue. Surely the devil overshot himself that time.

In the days of Esther the evil Haman listened to the blandishments of Satan and set out to try to destroy the Jews. The outcome revealed how very unwise the effort had been. The Jews went free and Haman swung from the very gallows he had erected for his hated enemy, the Jew Mordecai. When the body of Haman swung back and forth on the gallows he had built for another the folly of unrighteousness was exposed in a way and to a degree that must have surprised Satan. The world now knows, or can know if it will, that every gallows built to destroy good men will hang the builder at last. Justice may be a long time getting around to it, but evil will hang finally. Satan did not know this, or if he did he never intended that the secret should get out; either way his supposed shrewdness failed him.

Then, Satan's long, unrelenting warfare against the church has never been successful, and this has been at least partly due to his own unwisdom. In his fury he has shed the blood of millions of the saints, but always the blood of the martyr has become the seed of the church. "But the more they afflicted them, the more they multiplied and grew," first spoken of Israel, accurately describes conditions among the Christians down the centuries. Had Satan been the shrewd strategist he is said to be, he would long ago have stopped trying to exterminate Christianity by direct attack; yet he is still trying in many parts of the earth, and in so doing he is creating public sympathy for the very persons he is seeking to destroy. This reveals not wisdom but a large amount of blind malice instead.

For the Word of God and for the testimony of Jesus Christ the Apostle John was exiled to the lonely isle that is called Patmos and, if tradition may be believed, was sent to work in the mines. But from his mine John saw farther than any king ever saw from his throne; he saw more from his mine than any astronaut ever saw from his orbit, for the scroll of unborn history was spread out before him and he was permitted to see the unfolding of the purposes of God onward to the time when the New Jerusalem will descend out of heaven from God.

John would have been less trouble to the devil back in Ephesus. Had he been permitted to go quietly about his church duties he might have gotten comfortably old without giving the world a preview of the downfall of Satan's empire and his incarceration in the lake of fire. We can only conclude that Satan did not know how things would develop when he attacked John, and that he is therefore not as shrewd as he is supposed to be.

From Satan's standpoint the slaying of the Man Christ Jesus was another huge blunder. In his hatred he carried his persecution to the point where Jew and Gentile united to destroy this Man whose very presence was a rebuke and a judgment to them and to him. But God turned the cross into an altar, and while wicked men watched Jesus die in the belief that they were getting rid of Him for good, He through the Eternal Spirit was offering Himself without spot to God as an atoning sacrifice for the sins of the world. Surely this was never in the mind of Satan when he set out to kill the Man whom he instinctively knew was his great enemy. The resurrection of Christ was his most stunning defeat.

One thing we must never forget: Satan is too shrewd for any of us, and to trust to our wisdom is to take the sure way toward defeat. God has turned Satan's original wisdom into a built-in folly that makes it impossible for him to achieve his wicked ends. He has made evil his good, and in a moral world presided over by a just God, evil cannot win.

The Man and the Machine

Thoughts on seeing a man proudly driving a swank automobile:

He rode grandly by with arms stretched lovingly across the wheel, his nose slightly elevated and upon his face a look of utter content. He had achieved fulfillment. He was demonstrating before all worlds his reason for living. Here was nothing less than the Chief End of man.

One could not help but smile; yet the sight was not funny, for this man was representative of millions who, like him, have adopted a deeply erroneous and seriously damaging philosophy of life. If there were only one such man I might easily have missed the signs when thy but demonstrate the results of the steady, day-by-day, round-the-clock effort of the image-makers through every available medium of mass communication to make the man think what they want him to think.

Not the big car was bad, but the man's attitude toward it. What was intended to be a useful tool had been perverted into a symbol of superiority and a reason for existence. The whole thing takes on a religious character. The man is caught in a fallacy that cannot be shrugged off. It has its evil effects upon his present life and will shape his character for all time to come.

I have long ago given up the hope of making any appreciable change in the world's philosophy of life. Were I concerned solely with the ways of the world, this piece would never be written; but when the children of God accept the world's values it is time some Christian spoke up. Babylon may have her gods, her own way of life and her own moral standards. It is when Israel begins to adopt them, that the prophet of God becomes responsible to rise and cry against them.

The man in the big car is thinking wrongly about himself and others and everything that relates to himself and them. He is as completely wrong as a man who gets off a bus in London and believes himself to be in New York. For his error he must not be blamed or scolded for he is simply mistaken, terribly mistaken, and should be dealt with patiently as a lost man, for such he undoubtedly is, at least for the time.

Someone should explain to him that a man's life consisteth not in the abundance or elegance of the things which he possesseth. He should be taught that the excellence of anything lies in the perfection of its nature. The excellence of a horse (as Plato said somewhere) lies in the perfection of the qualities that make it a horse—strength, speed, intelligence, et cetera—and these cannot be transferred to something else. Give to a wren, for instance, the qualities that constitute a good horse and you have a grotesque monster that is neither wren nor horse. How unthinkable for a wren to perch on the back of the horse and ride proudly by under the mistaken impression that it has now reached his complete fulfillment. No. The horse cannot impart anything tot he nature of the wren that will add to its excellence as a wren. Let the wren know itself and seek its fulfillment singing beside its nest and gathering food for its young, not in trying to borrow a glory that must be forever foreign to it.

And so with a man. The excellence of a man lies in the perfection of his human nature. God made him with powers no other being possesses and gave him a physical body through which to express these powers fruitfully. An automobile has another and a different excellence; it can add nothing to the glory of the man.

Our Lord, riding into Jerusalem on the back of a humble beast, lost nothing of the majesty that was His as the world's most perfect man; conversely, a little, selfish, frightened man gains no dignity from the expensive and shiny steel monster in which he rides. That he feels greater only accents his feebleness; that he acts as if he were greater only reveals more clearly the basic error in his total life philosophy. He accepts as real the illusion that he is more powerful, when in fact the power lies outside of him. His imagined excellence is the excellence of a piece of machinery, something he must share with the little dog that sits beside him with his head out the window.

The whole point is that human excellence consists in the perfection of human nature. Things cannot enter men to make them better or more worthy. "A man can receive nothing, except it be given him from heaven." Only the God who made man's nature in the first place can remake it after the divine image.

A man's earthly situation can neither add to nor take from what the man has within him. The martyrs who went about in goatskins or hid from their tormentors in dens and caves of the earth had nothing external to support their self-confidence or give them social status. Yet in the great day of Christ their interior excellence will shine forth as the brightness of the sun.

So I watch the man drive proudly by and wonder why he does not understand that true excellence lies in moral character, not in the beauty or elegance of a soulless machine. And I wonder whether he is an unbeliever or a deacon in a nearby church. A gospel church perhaps. And my thoughts are troubled for myself, and mine, and those for whom I am responsible, and for all for whom Christ died.

41

Leaders and Followers

When our Lord called all of us sheep He told us that we should be followers, and when Peter called some of us shepherds he indicated that there should be among us leaders as well as followers.

Human nature being what it is, the need for leadership is imperative. Let five men be cast adrift in a lifeboat and immediately one of them assumes command. No plebiscite is necessary. Four of the men will know by a kind of intuition who the strong, wise man is, and without any formality he will take charge of things and become the leader.

Every disaster, every fire, every flood elects its own leaders. At such times the people listen without question to the man who has the presence of mind and the boldness to take command. In retrospect the weaker ones may find fault, but they were glad enough for the leadership when the crisis was on.

Among Christians too there are leaders and followers. The followers may resent the leader, but they need him nevertheless, and follow him too, even if a little sulkily sometimes.

The ideal would be that the sheep follow none but the Chief Shepherd and ignore all other leaders; and occasionally indeed an individualist is found who insists that he follows only the Lord and stubbornly refuses to listen to human teachers or to take part in the activities of the Christian community. While we respect the right of such a man to his own convictions, it must be said nevertheless that he is bound to be and to remain weak and fruitless. By detaching himself from the flock of the Lord he misses the green pastures and the still waters.

In the church of God there must be leaders; but the leader must also be a follower. Paul gave us the pattern when he exhorted the Corinthians, "Be ye followers of me, even as I also am of Christ" (1 Corinthians 11:1). To follow a leader who is faithfully following the Lord is to follow the Lord; to follow one who is not a follower of Christ is to end in disaster.

But how can we be sure? How can we know whom to trust? To the law and to the testimony! If the teacher speaks not according to God's Word there is no light in him. To follow a religious leader for his eloquence or his attractive personality is to travel on a very dangerous path. Many have done it to their everlasting sorrow and loss.

The true and safe leader is likely to be the one who has no desire to lead but is forced into a position of leadership by the inward pressure of the Spirit and the press of the external situation. Such were Moses, David and the Old Testament prophets; and I think there was hardly a great Christian leader from Paul to this present day but was drafted by the Holy Spirit for the task and commissioned by the Lord of the Church to fill a position he had little natural heart for.

I believe that it might be accepted as a fairly reliable rule of thumb that the man who is ambitious to lead is disqualified as a leader. The Church of the Firstborn is no place for the demagogue or the petty religious dictator. The true leader will have no wish to lord it over God's heritage, but will be humble, gentle, self-sacrificing and altogether as ready to follow as to lead when the Spirit makes it plain to him that a wiser and more gifted man than himself has appeared.

It is undoubtedly true, as I have said so often, that the church is languishing not for leaders but for the right kind of leaders; for the wrong kind is worse than none at all. Better to stand still than to follow a blind man over a precipice. History will show that the church has prospered most when blessed with strong leaders and suffered the greatest decline when her leaders were weak and time serving. The sheep rarely go much farther than the Shepherd.

That is why unqualified democracy is not good for a church unless every voting member is full of the Holy Spirit and wisdom. To put the work of the church in the hands of the group is to exchange one leader for many; and if the group is composed of carnal professors it is to exchange one weak leader for a number of bad ones. One hundred blind men cannot see any better than one.

The ideal leader is one who hears the voice of God and beckons the people on as the voice calls him and them. But unfortunately not all leaders are ideal ones. Too many lead by following. One of the most comical sights in the whole world of religious activities is to see an uncertain leader trying to discover the direction the people want him to lead them and then scrambling ahead of them trying to look like Moses on his way out of Egypt. Such a leader will send up a trial balloon and then boldly set out in the direction of the wind, doing his best to create the impression that the wind consulted him before it started to blow.

If this sounds harsh, let me insist that it is far short of the fact. Every city has its religious leader who enjoys a wide reputation as a prominent churchman but who never takes a position on anything until he has first read up on public opinion and is reasonably sure that he will be siding with the majority, or at least with the important minority. Such a man is a hireling and will be judged and disposed of as a hireling in the day of Christ.

We should pray that the Lord would send us leaders; and then we should pray for those leaders when they appear.

Other titles by A.W. Tozer available
through your local Christian bookstore:

The Attributes of God
The Attributes of God Journal
The Best of A.W. Tozer
Born after Midnight
The Christian Book of Mystical Verse
Christ the Eternal Son
The Counselor
The Early Tozer: A Word in Season
Echoes from Eden
Faith Beyond Reason
Gems from Tozer
God Tells the Man Who Cares
How to Be Filled with the Holy Spirit
I Call It Heresy!
I Talk Back to the Devil
Jesus, Author of Our Faith
Jesus Is Victor
Jesus, Our Man in Glory
Let My People Go, A biography of Robert A. Jaffray
Man: The Dwelling Place of God
Men Who Met God
The Next Chapter after the Last
Of God and Men
Paths to Power
The Price of Neglect
The Pursuit of God
The Pursuit of Man (formerly *The Divine Conquest*)
The Quotable Tozer
Renewed Day by Day, Vol. 1
Renewed Day by Day, Vol. 2
The Root of the Righteous
Rut, Rot or Revival
The Set of the Sail
The Size of the Soul

Success and the Christian
That Incredible Christian
This World: Playground or Battleground?
Tozer on Worship and Entertainment
The Tozer Pulpit 1
The Tozer Pulpit 2
The Tozer CD-ROM Library
Tozer Speaks to Students
Tozer Topical Reader
Tragedy in the Church: The Missing Gifts
A Treasury of A.W. Tozer
The Warfare of the Spirit
We Travel an Appointed Way
Whatever Happened to Worship?
Who Put Jesus on the Cross?
Wingspread, A biography of A.B. Simpson